Berlitz®

Lisbon

Front cover: Torre de Belém

Below: Monument to the Discoveries

Museu Nacional de Arte Antiga • Home to the city's finest art collection *(page 44)*

The Torre de Belém • This fine example of Manueline architecture guards the entrance to Lisbon *(page 51)*

Elevador de Santa Justa • A century-old iron lift with great city views *(page 36)*

Mosteiro dos Jerónimos • A jewel from Portugal's Golden Age *(page 47)*

Castelo de São Jorge • Built by the Moors, this castle is where present-day Portugal began (page 31)

Parque das Nações • Among the host of attractions here is a top-class aquarium (page 58)

Igreja do Carmo • This ruined church bears witness to the awful power of the 1755 earthquake (page 42)

The Bairro Alto • Bars, clubs and restaurants make the 'Upper City' Lisbon's centre of nightlife (page 40)

The Museu Gulbenkian • A superb and wide-ranging art collection (page 53)

The Alfama district • Narrow alleyways and red-roofed houses give a taste of medieval Lisbon (page 26)

CONTENTS

■ **Introduction** 7

■ **A Brief History** 13

■ **Where to Go** 25

A ➤ in the text denotes a highly recommended sight

Alfama 26

*Miradouros 26, Alfama Gems 28, São Vicente de
Fora and the Panteão Nacional 29, The Castle 31,
The Cathedral 32, A Detour East: Two Museums 33*

Baixa (Lower City) 35

Rossio 37

Bairro Alto (Upper City) 40

*Igreja de São Roque 41, Igreja do Carmo 42,
Chiado 43, São Bento 44*

Lapa 44

Belém 46

*Mosteiro dos Jerónimos 47, Padrão dos
Descobrimentos 50, Torre de Belém 51*

North Lisbon 52

*Estufa Fria 53, Museu Gulbenkian 53,
Aqueduto das Águas Livres 56*

Parque das Nações 58

Oceanário de Lisboa 58

Across the Tagus 61

Excursions from Lisbon.......................62

*Queluz 62, Sintra 64, Mafra 69, Estoril Coast 71,
South of Lisbon 75*

What to Do............................81

Shopping...81

Entertainment...................................85

Sports...88

Children's Activities.........................92

Eating Out...........................94

Handy Travel Tips..............104

Hotels and Restaurants........130

Index....................................143

Features

Lisboa Card...............................9
Inês and Pedro...........................14
Azulejos..................................18
Historical Landmarks..................23
St Vincent of Lisbon....................29
Manueline Architecture...............49
Calouste Gulbenkian..................54
Sintra's Country Market...............67
Fado......................................86
Calendar of Events.....................93
Port and Madeira......................102

32

38

80

INTRODUCTION

Lying with its back to Spain and its face to the Atlantic Ocean, Europe's most westerly country is about three-quarters the size of England. Around 2.5 million of its 10 million inhabitants live in Lisbon, the capital, which sits halfway down the coast on the estuary of the River Tagus (Tejo in Portuguese). The city is built over a number of hills on the right bank, facing south, at the estuary's narrowest point, where it shrinks to around 3km (2 miles). The largest bridges in Europe reach across to the expansive delta on the far side.

A few kilometres downriver from the city centre, just past the district of Belém, where Vasco da Gama and other discoverers of the Golden Age set out to explore the world, a lighthouse marks the point where the river ends

> **A global language**
>
> There are 220 million Portuguese speakers in the world, making it the eighth-largest language, and third-largest European language after English and Spanish.

and the Atlantic begins. The ocean defines the city: its limpid light turns to gold – a 'Straw Sea' – in the afternoon sun, and its fathomless, melancholic soul wells up in the music of *fado*.

Laid-Back Capital

Lisbon's great days are over, its colonies gone. Fortunes have risen and fallen dramatically over the course of its 3,000-year history. Even in recent times, a burst of economic activity that was sparked by the EU at the end of the 20th century has slipped back, and the city is quietly going about its business again. The truth seems to be that, in spite of its ability to shine in the modern world – especially for Expo 98

View towards the castle from the Elevador de Santa Justa

Tram above Alfama

in the cutting-edge Parque das Nações – Lisbon is really not too fond of the limelight. Instead it is content to enjoy a comfortable but slightly thread-bare, drawn-out retirement from its time as centre of empire and greatness.

Even when tourists began to arrive in any number, in the 20th century, Lisbon was seen as a lovely but laid-back provincial capital, known more for the charms of the narrow Moorish-style streets, the beauty of its hand-painted ceramic tiles and occasional ornate architectural flourishes than for economic dynamism. Today it is a modern, cosmopolitan city. Though a little shabby, it is exceedingly appealing, more notable for its understated beauty and easy friendliness than for world-class monuments or museums. With its neighbourhoods clustered on the sides of hills along the placid Tagus, there are gentle reminders everywhere of Lisbon's distant past: the Phoenician profile of the modern fishing boats; the Moorish expertise with painted tiles; the pained notes of *fado*'s longing and lament.

Streets and Viewpoints

The narrow whitewashed streets of the old Moorish neighbourhood, Alfama, twist and turn; they remain the heart of a modest, working-class, inner-city village. Here and elsewhere, Lisboetas decorate their balconies with flowerpots, their walls with colourful tiles, and the pavements with mosaics. Faded and frequently crumbling façades are festooned with lines of brightly coloured washing hung to dry. Building and restoration work is everywhere in evidence, but it is a slow and expensive business and there is a lot to do.

Local women carry bags of bread and groceries up and down Lisbon's hills without complaint, but visitors may prefer to opt for one of the charming century-old electric trams that still trundle through the city, or let one of the eccentric yellow funiculars take the strain. Wandering is rewarded with picturesque nooks or brilliant panoramic views of the city's red-tiled rooftops tumbling down towards the river. Whether from one of the lookouts in Alfama, the gardens of Castelo de São Jorge (St George's Castle) or the top of Santa Justa, the iron lift that used to transport workers and residents from the Baixa (lower) to the Bairro Alto (upper neighbourhood), Lisboetas never miss an opportunity to take in the whole of their city in its sun-kissed splendour.

Although the cold Atlantic lies only a few kilometres downriver, Lisbon feels decidedly Mediterranean. A sheltered, south-facing location and mild winters allow palm

Lisboa Card

Lisbon's tourist offices offer a discount Lisboa Card that entitles holders to free Metro (subway), bus, tram and lift transport; free entry into 27 museums and monuments; and discounts of between 10 and 50 percent in other places of interest, as well as discounts in some shops. The card (available for one, two or three days) covers nearly everything of interest to visitors, including sights outside Lisbon, such as the palaces in Sintra and Queluz.

Bird-of-paradise flower in
the Estufa Fria

trees and bird-of-paradise flowers to flourish, and the balmy weather encourages an unhurried pace. Lisboetas have a quiet, modest dignity and are the most gracious of hosts. The city's streets teem with people of diverse ethnicity and dress. Many are immigrants from Portugal's former African colonies – Angola, Cape Verde, Mozambique – or from Brazil, Macau and Goa, who arrived in Lisbon and soon founded their own little colonies, speaking a slightly softer version of the language and adding spice to the cuisine. Many newcomers from eastern Europe are here too.

Upper and Lower Districts

For the visitor, there may be fewer grand monuments than in many European capitals, but this makes sightseeing easier. The high point is St George's Castle, perched on top of Lisbon's loftiest hill. From its ramparts and quiet gardens with fabulous views, the castle overlooks Lisbon's oldest and most picturesque neighbourhood, Alfama. This working-class quarter, once home to the city's elite, survived the tremendous earthquake, but only the labyrinthine layout of the Moors remains.

To the west is the residential suburb of Belém, the city's most monumental district. It proclaims Portugal's Golden Age of Discovery with the finest Manueline monuments.

Between the two is the Baixa – 'lower', downtown Lisbon, a commercial waterfront district of neoclassical buildings, the old stock exchange and government ministries, quaint shops and grand squares. Most of the Baixa was lost to the natural disaster, but was quickly rebuilt on a grid pattern.

The upper city, the Bairro Alto, is reached by tram, lift or steep climb. One of Lisbon's quintessential neighbourhoods, it is home to much of the city's nightlife, including *fado* houses, restaurants and bars. Within the upper city is the chic district of Chiado. Though much of it was razed in 1988 by a devastating fire, it has been impeccably rebuilt and once again houses elegant shops.

Renovation work begun in the late 20th century has turned the city once again towards the river and the sea. The transport infrastructure continues to be improved. Old quays and warehouses have been transformed into trendy restaurants and hot nightspots, and the Parque das Nações has shifted the city's focus upriver.

Playing dominoes on Largo do Carmo

Photo opportunity in Sintra

Around the City

To experience the city as its residents do, you'll need to get out of town. Lisbon is surrounded by some of the country's most appealing spots, easy excursions by car or public transport. To the northwest, Sintra is one of the most delightful towns in Europe, with palaces and *quintas* (estates) lodged in beautiful pine-clad hills with views of the coast. To the west are the sparkling beach resorts of the Estoril Coast, while over the Tagus to the south are the wild Serra da Arrábida and the fishing town of Sesimbra. Closer to the capital, the handsome Versailles-style palace at Queluz is another major draw for visitors, including heads of state.

Food and Wine

Lisbon and its environs are best discovered at an unhurried pace. One of the great joys is Portuguese cuisine and wine, whether at a simple country inn or at one of Lisbon's chic designer restaurants and bars. Local cooking owes much to the country's close ties to the sea: fresh fish, seafood and soups hearty enough for a tired sailor's homecoming. One of the country's great secrets is its table wines, produced in every region. They're affordable, unpretentious and memorable – which is not a bad description of Lisbon itself.

A BRIEF HISTORY

Though a legend claims Odysseus as Lisbon's founding father, most hard-headed historians date the city's origins to around 1200BC, with the establishment of a Phoenician trading station. Its name then was Alis Ubbo or Olisipo.

People had settled in the area thousands of years before, attracted to its location on a calm river close to the Atlantic Ocean. Around 700BC, Celtic tribes moved into northern and central Portugal, while the coastal settlements were incorporated into the empire of Carthage.

Recorded history of the city begins in 205BC, when the Romans ousted the Carthaginians and created the province of Lusitania, though not without fierce resistance from the Celts. Olisipo was proclaimed a municipality and later renamed Felicitas Julia – the Joy of Julius – by Julius Caesar. The Romans built roads, cultivated grapes, wheat and olives, and bequeathed the foundations of the Portuguese language. As the power of Rome declined, most of the Iberian peninsula was overrun by tribes from north of the Pyrenees. Lisbon fell at the beginning of the 5th century AD, after which successive migratory tribes controlled the city until the Visigoths in the 6th century brought a period of peace.

The Moorish Conquest

In 711, 79 years after the death of the Prophet Mohammed, a great Muslim invasion fleet from North Africa crossed the Strait of Gibraltar, and in just a few years the Moors had conquered most of Iberia. Lisbon became a thriving outpost under Muslim rule. Its castle, begun by the Visigoths, was enlarged, and beneath it, tumbling down to the river, the narrow streets of Alfama were infused with an Arabic flavour that remains to this day.

Christians had maintained a precarious foothold in northern Portugal, and it was not until 1139, when Dom Afonso Henriques declared himself the first king of Portugal, that their struggle to gain power met with some success, defeating the Moors at the Battle of Ourique. However, Lisbon eluded his grasp for another eight years.

In 1147 the king recruited a volunteer force from thousands of Flemish, Norman, German and English crusaders on their way to the Holy Land, persuading them to strike a blow against the Moors in return for whatever booty Lisbon had to offer. The successful siege of Lisbon lasted four months. A century later the reconquest of Portugal was complete and Afonso III (1248–79) chose Lisbon as his capital.

The Golden Age

In a decisive battle, fought in 1385 at Aljubarrota (100km/ 62 miles north of Lisbon), João of Avis, recently proclaimed João I of Portugal, secured independence from Spain. A new alliance with England was sealed in the 1386 Treaty of Windsor, outlining true and eternal friendship. A year later King João married Philippa of Lancaster, the daughter of John of

Inês and Pedro

Inês de Castro and Pedro the Just are two tragic figures who could have served as the models for Shakespeare's Romeo and Juliet. Pedro, heir to the throne, defied his family and lived for a decade with the Spanish beauty, one of his queen's ladies-in-waiting. In 1355, three noblemen slit Inês's throat – a political assassination ordered by Prince Pedro's own father, Afonso IV. When he became king just two years later, Pedro exhumed her body, crowned it, and ordered all the nobles to kneel and kiss the skeleton's hand. Pedro and Inês are entombed together in the monastery at Alcobaça.

Gaunt. Their third surviving son, Henrique, Duke of Viseu, Master of the Order of Christ, became 'Henry the Navigator', who redrew the map of the world.

Prince Henry won his spurs in 1415 at the age of 21, when he sailed from Lisbon in a daring expedition to capture the North African stronghold of Ceuta. It was his first and last act of bravado, for he then retired to the 'end of the world', the Sagres peninsula in the Algarve, where he established a centre of research that gathered together astronomers, cartographers and other scientists whose work

Henry the Navigator

magnified the skills of mariners. Their expeditions redefined European understanding of the world. During Henry's lifetime, Portuguese caravels sailed far beyond the westernmost point of Africa. With the colonisation of the Atlantic islands of Madeira and the Azores, the foundations of the future Portuguese empire were swiftly laid.

The king who ruled over Portugal's Golden Age of Exploration – and exploitation – was Manuel I, 'The Fortunate', who reigned from 1495 to 1521. Discoveries made during this period made him one of Europe's richest rulers. During his reign the Tower of Belém and the impressive Jerónimos Monastery were built in the 'Manueline' architectural style that eased Portugal from the Gothic into the Renaissance.

Manueline style in the church at Jerónimos Monastery

Whimsically flamboyant and decorative, it is rife with references to the sea.

The most significant expedition under Manuel's flag was Vasco da Gama's sea voyage from Lisbon in the summer of 1497. Rounding what is now known as the Cape of Good Hope, Vasco da Gama found what Columbus had been looking for but missed – the sea route to the spices of the East. Reaching Calicut in southern India the following year, Portugal put an end to the Venetian monopoly of the Eastern spice trade by assuming control of the Indian Ocean and attracting merchants from all over Europe to Lisbon. Further territories were discovered in 1500, when the Portuguese explorer Pedro Álvares Cabral reached Brazil.

Times of Trial

When Manuel died in 1521, he was succeeded by his son, João the Pious. With one eye on the ungodly ways of prosperous Lisbon and the other on the Inquisition in Spain, João invited the Jesuits to cross the border into Portugal.

Although the Inquisition in Portugal was never as powerful as it was in Spain, it relentlessly persecuted 'New Christians' – Jews who were all forced to embrace Christianity, including Spanish Jews who had been promised refuge in Portugal. Despite these witch hunts, an outbreak of plague and such natural calamities as earthquakes, by the end of the 16th century Lisbon had an estimated population of 100,000.

However, hard times followed and many left to find a better life in the new colonies. When Dom Henrique died leaving no heir in 1580, Philip II of Spain marched in and forced the union of the two crowns. It took 60 years for the local forces to organise a successful uprising against the occupation. On 1 December 1640 – celebrated as Portugal's Restoration Day – Spanish rule was finally overthrown, and the Duke of Bragança was crowned João IV in a joyful ceremony in Lisbon's huge riverfront square, the Terreiro do Paço, known as the Praça do Comércio today.

His grandson, João V, enjoyed a long and glittering reign, from 1706 to 1750. As money poured in from gold discovered in Brazil, the king squandered it on lavish monuments and buildings. His greatest extravagance was the palace and monastery at Mafra, 40km (25 miles) northwest of the capital.

Destruction and Rebuilding

The great divide between Portugal's early history and modern times falls around the middle of the 18th century when, on All Saints' Day, 1 November 1755, as the crowds packed the churches to honour the dead, Lisbon was devastated by one of the worst earthquakes ever recorded. Churches crumbled, the waters of the Tagus heaved into a tidal wave and fires spread throughout the city. The triple disaster is estimated to have killed between 15,000 and 60,000. Reminders of the nightmare are still found across Lisbon; the most evocative is the shell of the Carmelite church in the Bairro Alto district behind the Elevador de Santa Justa, which has been open to the sky since the morning its roof fell in.

Routine problems of state were beyond the talents of the ineffectual José I (1750–77), who could not be expected to cope with the challenge of post-quake recovery. The task of rebuilding fell to the power behind the throne – a tough, ambitious and tyrannical minister, Sebastião José de Carvalho e Melo, later Count of Oeiras, but best remembered as the Marquês de Pombal. Taking advantage of the power vacuum once the earth had stopped shaking, he mobilised all of Portugal's resources for the clean-up. Survivors were fed and housed, corpses disposed of, ruins cleared and an ambitious project for a newly structured city laid out.

Today, the modern sections of the capital are aptly referred to as 'Pombaline Lisbon'. Pombal's achievements are commemorated with his heroic statue, on top of a column at the north end of the Avenida da Liberdade in downtown Lisbon, a central road hub referred to as 'Pombal'. A huge equestrian statue of José holds the main place of honour in the Praça do Comércio where the riverside royal palace had been before the earthquake. The king had a close brush with death in an assassination attempt in 1758, after which Pombal inaugurated a reign of terror, with widespread repression.

Azulejos

Azulejos, the hand-painted, glazed ceramic tiles omnipresent in Lisbon, are not merely decorative. After the Great Earthquake and fires devastated much of Lisbon and the surrounding area in the 18th century, these tiles were widely used to protect buildings from going up in flames again. The name *azulejo* is thought to be derived from *al-zuleiq*, Arabic for small polished stone. At the Museu Nacional do Azulejo you can see how they are made.

Tile panel at Miradouro de Santa Luzia, showing Lisbon's royal palace before the earthquake

The Peninsular War

At the beginning of the 19th century, Napoleon managed to drag Portugal into the heat of Europe's conflicts. The situation became so perilous that the royal family fled to Brazil on board British ships. Taking no chances, they remained there until 1821, 10 years after the crisis was over.

In 1807 Napoleon had tried to pressure Portugal into abandoning its traditional loyalty to England. Lisbon attempted to stay neutral, but when it refused to declare war on Britain, the French army under General Andoche Junot marched in, setting up headquarters in the Queluz Palace, just outside Lisbon.

Military miscalculations in the face of a British expedition sent Junot's army packing in 1808. Over the next few years, repeat engagements became notable victories for the combined Portuguese-British forces, who owed much to the strategic brilliance of the great British commander, Sir Arthur Wellesley (later the Duke of Wellington). After the textbook battle of the Lines of Torres Vedras, north of Lisbon, the French began a long retreat, sacking and looting as they went. Their last outpost in Portugal was evacuated in 1811.

Civil War

Peace was still to prove elusive, and 17 years later the country was again at war – this time pitting brother against brother. On the death of João VI, his eldest son, Pedro IV, who had become emperor of a newly independent Brazil, fought to wrest the crown of Portugal from his absolutist brother, Miguel I. Pedro won, though he died of consumption only months later, in September 1834, aged 36. His adolescent daughter, Maria da Glória, assumed the throne. She married the German nobleman Ferdinand of Saxe-Coburg-Gotha, who built for her the astonishing Pena Palace above Sintra and fathered her five sons and six daughters. Maria II died in childbirth at the age of 34.

Premature and tragic deaths claimed many Portuguese royals, but in all the country's history only one

Statue of Pedro IV in the Rossio

king was assassinated. On 1 February 1908, as the royal family was riding in an open carriage past the Terreiro do Paço, an assassin's bullet felled Carlos I. A few seconds later another conspirator fatally shot Carlos's son and heir, Prince Luís Felipe. A third bullet hit the young prince Manuel in the arm. Thus wounded and haunted, Manuel II began a brief two-year reign as Portugal's last king. He was deposed on 5 October 1910 in a republican uprising supported by certain elements of the armed forces. The royal yacht spirited him to Gibraltar and later to England, where he lived in exile.

Republic to Dictatorship

The republican form of government was as unstable as it was unfamiliar. Resignations, coups and assassinations kept an unhappy merry-go-round of presidents and prime ministers whirling. The nation could ill afford a war, but German threats to its African territories pushed Portugal towards World War I on the side of the Allies. On 24 February 1916, the Portuguese navy seized a group of German ships anchored in the Tagus, and the Kaiser replied with the inevitable declaration of war. A Portuguese expeditionary force sailed for the trenches of France.

The war's toll hastened the end of Portugal's unsuccessful attempt at democracy. After a revolution in 1926, General António Óscar Carmona assumed control, and two years later entrusted the economy to António de Oliveira Salazar, then an economics professor at Coimbra University. The exhausted Portuguese finances rallied soon afterwards. In 1932 Salazar was named prime minister. His tough, authoritarian regime – the Estado Novo (New State) – favoured economic progress and nationalism. He kept Portugal neutral in World War II, but permitted the Allies to use the Azores as a base.

The Carnation Revolution

When Salazar suffered a stroke in 1968, power was handed to Dr Marcelo Caetano. However, in 1974 the armed forces, discontented by hopeless colonial wars, overthrew the dictatorship in the so-called Carnation Revolution. Portugal disengaged itself from Mozambique and Angola, and managed to absorb the million or so refugees who fled to a motherland most had never seen. The nation suffered several years of political confusion and great hardship before adjusting to democracy.

Lisbon of the future at Estação do Oriente

With entry into the European Union in 1986, development quickened, and Portugal soon had one of Europe's fastest-growing economies. As host of World Expo in 1998, Lisbon launched a gleaming new neighbourhood, Parque das Nações, east of the city. That year too saw the writer José Saramago win the Nobel Prize for Literature. In 2004 Portugal hosted the European Football Championship for which new stadiums were built, others renovated. But the economy began to stagnate and governments changed. In February 2005 the Social Democrats lost power to the Socialists, who won their first overall majority. In 2007 the Portuguese voted in a referendum to legalise abortion, changing tradition for ever in this overwhelmingly Roman Catholic country.

Historical Landmarks

c.1200BC Phoenicians establish Alis Ubbo or Olisipo trading post.
c.700BC Celtic tribes arrive.
205BC Romans create Lusitania; Olisipo is made a municipality.
5th century AD After the decline of Rome, Visigoths settle in Lisbon.
711 Moors arrive on the peninsula and swiftly conquer it.
883 Northern Portugal (Portucale) regained by Christian forces.
1139 Dom Afonso Henríques declares himself first king of Portugal.
1147 Lisbon taken by Afonso Henríques.
1255 Capital of Portugal transferred from Coimbra to Lisbon.
1386 Treaty of Windsor confirms England–Portugal alliance.
1415 Explorers reach Madeira, starting the Age of Discoveries.
1498 Vasco da Gama opens a sea route to India.
1500 Pedro Álvares Cabral reaches Brazil.
1502 Construction of Jerónimos Monastery begins.
1536 Inquisition introduced.
1580 Portugal falls under Spanish rule for 60 years.
1755 The Great Earthquake devastates Lisbon.
1807 Napoleonic troops invade Portugal at the start of the Peninsular War; royal family leaves for Brazil.
1828–34 Civil war between Pedro IV and Miguel I.
1834 Religious orders dissolved and church property seized.
1908 Carlos I and Prince Luís Felipe assassinated.
1916 Germany declares war on Portugal.
1932 António de Salazar becomes prime minister and effective dictator.
1974 The Carnation Revolution restores democracy; Portugal pulls out of African colonies and a million expatriates return.
1986 Portugal joins the European Union.
1998 Expo 98 transforms Lisbon's eastern waterfront.
2001 The euro replaces the escudo as the national currency.
2004 Lisbon hosts the European Football Championship finals.
2005 Socialists win elections and their first overall majority.
2007 Portuguese vote to legalise abortion.

WHERE TO GO

Lisbon's waterfront is an arc stretching nearly 32km (20 miles) along the River Tagus (Tejo in Portuguese). At the western end is Belém and at the eastern extreme is the Parque das Nações, the site of Expo 98. A map shows that many of the top attractions in Lisbon are within walking distance of the river, but because of the hills and the way in which the sights are spread out, it isn't always very easy to go directly from one to the other.

As in many cities, it's best to organise your time and interests according to neighbourhood. The Belém district on the west side of the city holds several of the star visitor attractions, but the central areas, such as Alfama and the Bairro Alto either side of the Baixa, are better for dining, shopping and lingering.

The Tagus

The River Tagus (Tejo) is 940km (585 miles) long, rising in Spain (where it is known as the Rio Tajo), and passing through Toledo. Its delta, to the south of Lisbon, is an important wildlife area.

You can travel cheaply and efficiently from place to place by public transport. Buses are quick and straightforward. Antique trams ply routes around the old town, and funiculars climb steep hills. Lisbon's Metro system is modern and fast, but serves a limited area, though expansion is underway. Taxis are plentiful and fairly inexpensive. Parking is usually difficult or even impossible on weekdays, so a car is best saved for out-of-town excursions.

On arrival, a guided city tour, whether by bus or ferry along the river, can be a good way to grasp the general layout *(see page 117)*.

Elevador de Santa Justa

ALFAMA

Alfama is Lisbon's oldest, most picturesque and fascinating area. Here, in a labyrinth of steep, crooked streets, alleys and stairways – a layout left by Moorish occupants of the city – little seems to have changed since the Middle Ages. The whole area between the castle and the waterfront is a jumble of tilting houses with peeling paint, pastel laundry hanging from windows, bars and fish stalls. The streets are so narrow that it's not uncommon to overhear elderly women sharing gossip across balconies.

You are almost certain to get lost, but in this area – safe and easygoing by day – that's part of the attraction. Stick to the narrow streets; if you find yourself in a street wide enough for two cars to pass, then you have strayed from the Alfama area.

A good start to your explorations is at the bottom of the hill at the **Casa do Fado e da Guitarra Portuguesa** (Fado and Guitar Museum; open daily 10am–6pm; admission fee) in Largo do Chafariz de Dentro. This sets the tone for the soul of the district, with a history of the city's famous music in song sheets, film clips and recordings, and a complete mocked-up *fado* tavern where you can sit and listen to Amália Rodrigues and other bygone stars, then select a souvenir from the CDs on sale.

Trams to Alfama

Taking a tram is the best way to get up into Alfama: No. 12 goes from Praça da Figueira, No. 28 from Bairro Alto. They share the same tracks in Alfama and you won't get lost if you follow their iron rails.

Miradouros

Alternatively, take the easier path into Alfama, with a tram to one of its vantage points, and let gravity lead you back down towards the river. The **Miradouro de Santa Luzia** is one such

The rootops of Alfama and the Tagus

bluff on the edge of Alfama. From a pretty balcony covered with painted tiles and bougainvillea there are stunning views over a jumble of tiled roofs that cascade down to the river. Tourists mix with old men in black berets playing cards and chatting. Two detailed and dramatic *azulejos* (tile panels) on the wall facing the belvedere show Lisbon's waterfront as it was before the Great Earthquake *(see page 19)* and, in blood-thirsty detail, the rout of the Moors from the castle.

Just up the street is another terrific *miradouro* (lookout point), with even more expansive views. A small café on **Largo das Portas do Sol** serves snacks and beverages; visitors have been known to remain here for hours on end.

Between the two, just above the Miradouro de Santa Luzia, the handsome 17th-century **Azurra Palace** has been filled with choice pieces of furniture, ceramics, silver, carpets and tapestries from 16th- to 19th-century Portugal and its colonies, forming the **Museu de Artes Decorativas** (Decorative Arts

Museum; open Tues–Sun 10am–5pm; admission fee). The museum belongs to the Ricardo do Espírito Santo Silva Foundation, which was established in the 1950s by the banker of the same name. The Foundation has 18 workshops devoted to woodwork, metalwork, bookbinding and other traditional crafts.

Alfama Gems

Some of Alfama's lesser-known attractions are best stumbled across by accident, through an arch or around a blind corner. Here is a selection of them.

Narrow alleyway in Alfama

Rua de São João da Praça is where the first king of Portugal, Dom Afonso Henriques, entered Lisbon through the Moorish defensive wall on 25 October 1147. The remains of a tower that was part of the Moorish defences can be found on **Largo de São Rafael**.

Rua de São Pedro is Alfama's boisterous main shopping street and site of a fish market. On weekday mornings, fish-wives shriek amidst a cacophony of chickens, dogs and children playing football.

Igreja de São Miguel (St Michael's Church) was built in the 12th century and restored after the earthquake; it has a glorious ceiling of Brazilian jacaranda wood and a rococo gilt altar screen. To the east, **Igreja de Santo Estêvão** (St Stephen's Church) has a 13th-century octagonal floor plan, but has been rebuilt several times over the years; the overhanging back of the church nearly collides with the front gate of an old palace.

The alley called **Beco da Cardosa**, with its blind-alley off-shoots, is the very essence of Alfama's appeal. On **Beco do Carneiro** (Sheep Alley), ancient houses sag towards each other across a step-street barely wide enough for two people; above, the eaves of the buildings actually touch.

São Vicente de Fora and the Panteão Nacional

Just beyond the dense quarters of the Alfama, but linked to the neighbourhood, are two of its top sights. Though you might have trouble navigating the crooked streets up to it, the twin towers of **Igreja e Mosteiro de São Vicente de Fora** (Church and Monastery of St Vincent Beyond the Walls), rising above a hillside east of the São Jorge castle, are impossible to miss. Founded by Dom Afonso Henríques immediately after retaking the city from the Moors (tombs of the Teutonic knights who helped him lie beneath the Sacristy), it was reconstructed in the 16th century around the time of the Inquisition. This huge Italianate building

St Vincent of Lisbon

The remains of St Vincent are kept in a beautiful silver reliquary at São Vicente de Fora. Vincent was martyred at Valencia in 336, but when the Moors took that city in the 8th century the inhabitants fled by sea, taking the relics of St Vincent with them. They were driven ashore on the coast of Algarve at the cape now known as Cape St Vincent, and there the relics remained until Dom Afonso Henriques had them brought to the capital and deposited in the church he had just built. Two ravens faithfully escorted the saintly relics, which explains why many a Lisbon lamp-post bears the symbol of a sailing ship with a bird fore and aft.

Thieves' Market

Behind São Vicente, around the Mercado Santa Clara, Alfama's colourful *Feira da Ladra* (Thieves' Market) is held every Tuesday and Saturday from dawn to dusk.

succeeds in combining mass with grace. The entrance to the **monastery** (open daily 9am–12.30pm, 3–6pm; admission fee) is on the right, where there is a pleasant café. Built over an enormous cistern, many of the monastery's walls and courtyards are lined with *azulejos*, though the *Fables* of La Fontaine, depicted in 38 *azulejo* tableaux, have been removed and repositioned for display on the first floor. An exhibition explains the history of the Patriarchate of Lisbon, granted by the Pope in 1720, and pantheons contain tombs of the patriarchs and of Bragança royalty, including Catherine of Bragança, queen of Charles II of England, and Carlos I and his heir Prince Luís Felipe, assassinated together in 1908.

A further pantheon, the **Panteão Nacional** (Igreja de Santa Engrácia) is the other dominant building in the area, located just downhill from the monastery. This grandiosely domed marble church was begun in the 17th century, but the final touch, the cupola, wasn't completed until 1966. Describing something as the 'works of Santa Engrácia' is calling it an endless task.

Santa Engrácia remained a church until a few years ago, when it was deconsecrated and became the national pantheon, honouring great figures in Portuguese history with symbolic tombs in the sumptuous rotunda. To one side are the real tombs of presidents of the republic and contibutors to Portuguese culture, including the famous *fado* singer Amália Rodrigues (1920–99), which always has fresh flowers. You can climb to the gallery for a view onto the marble floor of the rotunda, and to the terrace and dome, though there is often a queue for the lift.

The Castle

Almost every hill in this elevated part of town has a *mira-douro*, but the best panorama of all belongs to the **Castelo de São Jorge** (St George's Castle; open daily summer 9am–9pm, winter 10am–6pm; admission fee), which is reached by the steep alley and steps that continue up from the tram stop on Rua de Santa Justa. From the ramparts, you can look out across the centre of Lisbon, over the Baixa to the Bairro Alto, down to the river and the Ponte 25 de Abril, as far as Belém.

The Moors, who ruled Portugal between the 8th and 12th centuries, clung hard to their castle but were finally dislodged in 1147. The new proprietor, Dom Afonso Henriques, expanded the fortifications, but earthquakes as well as general wear and tear over the following centuries left little intact. Restoration has since given new life to the old ruins, even if that means that much of the castle is not original.

The Castelo de São Jorge

Apart from the sensational vistas and the chance to roam the battlements, the castle is worth a visit for the park gardens inside its walls. Peacocks and other birds strut around as if they own the place. There is a café and restaurant in the castle, and souvenir shops are to hand. **Olisipónia** is a 30-minute multimedia history of Lisbon.

The Cathedral

Many cities are built around their grand cathedral squares, but Lisbon's cathedral, the **Sé Patriarcal**, appears out of nowhere at a bend in the road. It is most easily reached from the centre by continuing east on the extension of Rua da Conceição. Despite the lack of pomp and circumstance, this handsome building has significant historic and artistic importance. Begun as a fortress-church in the 12th century, its towers and walls suggest a citadel. The church suffered earthquake damage during the 14th, 16th and 18th centuries, but it retains its Romanesque façade. The 13th-century cloister gardens (open daily 9am–5pm; admission fee) have been excavated to reveal signs of Iron Age, Roman and Moorish occupation all on this same site. A **Roman amphitheatre** has been uncovered just above the site.

The cathedral's west front

A few steps down the hill from the cathedral, the little **Igreja de Santo António da Sé**, built in 1812, honours Lisbon's revered native son. Known throughout the world as St Anthony of Padua, to Lisboetas he is Santo António de Lisboa. The crypt – all that survived the 1755 earthquake – was built on the spot where, according to local lore, St Anthony's house stood. He is the patron saint of women looking for husbands; some-

Casa dos Bicos

times bridal bouquets are left at his altar in the cathedral, along with thanks for all of his good work. Pope John Paul II prayed in the crypt during his 1982 visit to Lisbon.

Towards the waterfront, at Campo das Cebolas, the **Casa dos Bicos** is worth noting. The building, faced with sharp pyramid-shaped stones, was built during the early 16th century, and belonged to the illegitimate son of Afonso de Albuquerque, the viceroy of Portuguese India.

The **Rua dos Bacalhoeiros** (Street of Cod-Sellers), on which the house stands, has various small *tascas* (restaurants) and the Loja dos Descobrimentos handicraft shop, special-ising in hand-painted tiles. The west end of the street leads to the busy waterfront square, Praça do Comércio.

A Detour East: Two Museums

Along the riverfront just to the east of Alfama are two important museums. The **Museu Militar** (Military Museum; open Tues–Sun 10am–5pm; admission fee), located in a large

Praça do Comércio

building across the square from the Santa Apolónia railway station, is on the site of a foundry where cannons were cast during the 16th century. Among the exhibits is Henry the Navigator's two-handed sword, almost as tall as a man, relics of the Napoleonic Wars and mementoes of Portugal's last skirmishes in its colonies.

A short way beyond is the **Museu Nacional do Azulejo** (National Tile Museum; open Tues–Sun 10am–5pm; admission fee), devoted entirely to the art of the painted ceramic tiles that are on view everywhere in Portugal. The museum occupies much of the former Manueline Convento da Madre de Deus (1509), and includes a small double-decker cloister surrounded by tiles in Moorish-style geometric patterns. About 12,000 *azulejos* are on show, from 15th-century polychrome designs to contemporary examples.

One treasure is the *Lisbon Panorama*, a 36m- (118ft-) long composition of blue-and-white painted tiles, recording Lisbon's riverside as it looked 25 years before the 1755 earthquake. Another is the fabulous interior of the small church of Igreja da Madre de Deus, a heady mix of rococo gilt and gorgeous *azulejos*. Side walls are adorned with blue-and-white tiles from Holland; two rows of enormous paintings hang above them, and the ceiling also serves as a giant canvas.

BAIXA (LOWER CITY)

Praça do Comércio (Commerce Square) is a rare extravagant touch in understated Lisbon. Stately arcades and bold yellow government buildings line all three sides of the vast square; the fourth is open to the river, with Venetian-style marble stairs leading down to the water. On the east side of the stairs is the Terreiro do Paço terminal for ferries to the opposite shore and for river cruises in summer *(see page 117)*. Ferries also leave from Cais do Sodré to the west.

Terreiro do Paço (Palace Square) was the name of this square during the four centuries when the Royal Palace stood

No Metro

Though central to the city, Praça do Comércio has no Metro station. Recent plans to build one have been thwarted by a combination of impregnable granite bedrock and invading river water.

on it, and many Lisboetas still use this name today, but the 1755 earthquake wiped out the entire complex of palatial buildings. The post-quake layout is harmonious and stately, but it remains part of many citizens' daily lives. They catch buses and trams here, while children play around temporary exhibitions and installations.

The Praça do Comércio has been the backdrop for some of history's dramas: King Carlos I and his son were killed by an assassin here in 1908, and this is where the first uprising of the Carnation Revolution of 1974 was staged.

On the west side, at Rua do Arsenal 15, is the **Lisboa Welcome Centre**, the city's main tourist office. In the middle of the square is the bronze equestrian statue of José I, patron of the Marquês de Pombal, who designed the square as the centrepiece of his post-earthquake resconstruction. Another sculptural flourish is the triumphal arch, depicting the Marquês de Pombal and the explorer Vasco da Gama, and connecting government buildings on the north of the square.

The arch leads to the pedestrianised **Rua Augusta**, the main thoroughfare of Pombal's 18th-century grid and an attractive shopping street. Tiled façades and Art Nouveau touches are a feature of these 15 earthquake-proof side streets, which are full of intriguing shops, banks and small restaurants. The parallel Rua de Prata and Rua do Ouro (Silver and Gold Streets) are named after the original specialist shops in the area.

On the west side of the Baixa is the Bairro Alto, the 'Upper Quarter', which was once easily scaled by the **Elevador de Santa Justa**, a 30m- (100ft-) high iron neo-Gothic lift built by Raúl Mesnier in 1902. Originally powered by steam, it was rebuilt in 1993, but the upper gangway that gave access to the Bairro Alto proved unsafe and is now blocked off. Today the still-functioning lift takes people to the level just below the top, from where a spiral staircase leads up to the main observation deck with its pleasant café and sensational views of Lisbon's tiled rooftops and the São Jorge castle.

The steps behind the lift lead up to emerge at the gently sloping **Rua do Carmo**, with its blend of modern and traditional shops. The latter include the **Luvaria Ulisses**, a glove shop whose street frontage is barely a metre wide.

Rossio

Turn left up Rua do Carmo to enter the Chiado district *(see page 43)*, or follow it down to the right to emerge on the **Rossio** (formally named Praça Dom Pedro IV), Lisbon's main square, once the scene of public hangings, bullfights and the

The Rossio viewed from the Elevador de Santa Justa

burning of the Inquisition's victims. Today, the square is still one of the main centres of activity in Lisbon – it's a great place to window-shop, meet friends, watch the busy crowds go by from pavement cafés, such as the Art Nouveau **Nicola**, and listen to the fountains and the cries of the newsboys and flower sellers. It is also a popular place to catch a taxi or bus.

The statue on the column in the square honours the first emperor of Brazil, Pedro IV (1826–34). On the northern end of the square is the handsome **Teatro Nacional Dona Maria II**. Just beyond the theatre on the right are a couple of *ginjinha* (cherry brandy) kiosks, which make the area an evening gathering place. Nearby is the southern end of **Rua das Portas de Santo Antão**, a street bustling with lively restaurant tables appreciated by patrons of the popular **Teatro Politeama** up on the left. At No. 58 is the **Casa do Alentejo**. Once the property of the counts of Alverca, this

Fountain in the Rossio

is now the regional house of the residents of the Alentejo region, to the east of Lisbon. It looks quite unassuming from the outside, but as you go through the entrance and up the steps you're confronted by a riot of interior styling: a Moorish courtyard with Art Deco flourishes, and on the first floor a restaurant with massed panels of vivid *azulejos*, serving excellent Alentejo dishes at a reasonable price.

On the west side of the square, one street removed, is the **Estação do Rossio**, the railway station where local trains run to Sintra and Mafra *(see pages 64–71)*. Its horseshoe arches make it look like a Moorish palace, but it is a romantic effort of the late 19th century.

To the east of Rossio is another major square, **Praça da Figueira**, which is another hub for buses – and the No. 12 tram. At its centre is a statue of João I, founder of the Avis dynasty. Just to the northeast is **Praça Martim Moniz**, decked with fountains that function as a water park for children, modern steel kiosks with handicrafts and other small enterprises. The views of Alfama and the castle district from here are lovely.

The road past Rossio station opens out into **Praça dos Restauradores** (Square of the Restoration), where an obelisk celebrates the overthrow of Spanish rule in 1640. **Palácio Foz**, the once splendid pink palace on the west side of the square beside the former Art Deco Teatro Eden, now houses a **tourist information office** for both the city and the country. Just beyond it, the Elevador da Glória funicular takes you up to the Bairro Alto *(see page 40)*.

From this point, **Avenida da Liberdade** makes its way uphill for a little over 1km (½ mile). The stately boulevard of upmarket shops is graced with statues, fountains, ponds, flower gardens, promenade cafés and benches. The boulevard ends at the **Praça Marquês de Pombal** (or Rotunda) traffic hub from which an elevated statue of Pombal, accompanied by a lion, looks out over his rebuilt Lisbon.

Evening time in the Bairro Alto

BAIRRO ALTO (UPPER CITY)

Like the steep Alfama district, the Bairro Alto is a hilly and dense area full of picturesque old houses, their wrought-iron balconies hung with birdcages and flowerpots. The Bairro Alto is the nightlife epicentre of Lisbon. At night the sad songs of *fado* nightclubs spill out into the streets, as do bohemian revellers who bop from one disco or bar to another.

The easiest way to reach the Bairro Alto is to board the **Elevador da Glória**, the yellow funicular trolley at Praça dos Restauradores. Locals, however, are as apt to walk up the hill as wait for the funicular. At the top end of the brief journey is a lookout park, **Miradouro de São Pedro de Alcântara**, with an excellent view of the Castelo de São Jorge across the Baixa.

Opposite the top of the funicular, on the ground floor of the 1717 Palace of São Pedro de Alcântara, is the **Solar do Vinho do Porto** (Port Wine Institute; open Mon–Fri 11am–midnight,

Sat 2pm–midnight), where you can sample the famous port wines in the comfort of an armchair, served by waiters.

North of the *miradouro*, along Rua de São Pedro de Alcântara, lies the **Jardim Botânico** (Botanical Garden), reached through the university gate alongside the Academy of Sciences. It concentrates on the scientific cultivation of unusual plants from distant climes, but this serious activity doesn't disturb the lush, slightly unkempt beauty and tranquillity. The tree-shaded gardens slope steeply downhill to a lower gate near the Avenida Metro station.

Igreja de São Roque

Two churches in the upper town are unusual enough to merit a visit. Just down Rua de São Pedro do Alcântara, turning left from the top of the funicular, is Largo Trindade Coelho and the **Igreja de São Roque**. The church's dull exterior (the original 16th-century façade perished in the 1755 earthquake) conceals the most lavishly decorated chapel in Lisbon: the baroque altar of the chapel of São João Baptista (St John the Baptist) is a wealth of gold, silver, bronze, agate, amethyst, lapis lazuli, ivory and Carrara marble. In 1742, João V of Portugal sent orders for this altar to Rome, where teams of artists and artisans worked on it for five years. After the Pope had given his blessing, the prefabricated masterpiece was dismantled and shipped to the customer. The church ceiling, from 1589, is the only surviving example in Lisbon of a Mannerist painted ceiling. Adjoining the church, the

Chapel of São João Baptista in the Igreja de São Roque

Museu de Arte Sacra (Museum of Sacred Art; open Tues–Sun 10am–5pm; admission fee) contains a collection of precious reliquaries, delicately worked jewellery and vestments.

The Bairro Alto's restaurants and bars are located in the side streets to the west of Rua de São Pedro de Alcântara. For a daylight impression of the narrow streets with their over-hanging balconies, take a walk from Largo Trindade Coelho up the **Travessa da Queimada**. The streets are in a grid pattern, so it's easy to explore and navigate your way back.

From Largo Trindade Coelho, you can also walk down-hill towards the Chiado district, via **Rua Nova da Trindade**. Halfway down on the left is the **Cervejeria da Trindade**, an old beer hall decorated with *azulejos*, where you can enjoy hearty food (the sea-food is excellent) at reasonable prices *(see page 137)*.

Igreja do Carmo

Igreja do Carmo

If you continue to the bottom and turn left, you'll arrive at Largo do Carmo, where the **Igreja do Carmo** (Carmelite Church) is rich only in memories. Today it stands in ruins, a mere shell, but an evocative reminder of the 1755 earthquake's tremendous destruction – the roof fell in on a full congregation on All Saints' Day. The foundations date to the 14th century. Housed inside the only part of the church that has a roof over it is the **Museu Archeológico do Carmo** (open Mon–Sat 10am–5pm; admission fee). This small archaeological museum has a collection that includes prehistoric pottery, some Roman sculptures, early Portuguese tombs and even a few ancient mummies under glass.

Chiado

The streets of chic **Chiado** have long been renowned for dispensing Lisbon's most elegant goods – silverware, leather, fashions and books

Statue of poet Fernando Pessoa outside Café A Brasileira

– along with fine pastry and tea shops. The main commerical street, with some high-end fashion shops, is **Rua Garrett**, where a statue of the poet Fernando Pessoa sits outside **Café A Brasileira**, which has attracted artists for a century.

In 1988 part of Chiado was devastated by fires that wiped out two of Europe's oldest department stores, including the legendary Armazéns do Chiado. Portugal's most famous architect, the modernist Álvaro Siza, oversaw the tastefully preserved reconstruction of the neighbourhood, especially along Rua do Carmo (see page 37). The local fire brigade is based in the **Largo Barão Quintela**, just off Rua do Alecrim, and here there is another statue, this one of the 19th-century novelist Eça de Queiroz, gazing upon a naked muse.

The **Museu do Chiado** (open Wed–Sun 10am–6pm, Tues 2–6pm; admission fee), in the former San Francisco Convent on Rua Serpa Pinto, is a major exhibition space for contemporary art.

São Bento

West of the Bairro Alto lies the **Palácio São Bento**, a former Benedictine monastery that houses Portugal's parliament. Beyond it is the delightful park Jardim Guerra
Jumqueiro, better known as **Jardim da Estrela** after the dis-
tinguished 18th-century church across the street. This rich-
ly decorated basilica was completed in 1789. The
19th-century park contains abundant tropical foliage, plus
the customary ducks, geese, peacocks and pheasants. Just
beyond the park is the **Cemitério dos Ingleses** (English
Cemetery), where Henry Fielding (1707–54), author of *Tom
Jones*, is buried.

LAPA

Moving west and down towards the river from Chiado is
the elegant residential neighbourhood of Lapa. It is home
to embassies, townhouses and several intimate hotels, but
to most visitors it is known as the address of the **Museu
Nacional de Arte Antiga** (National Museum of Ancient
Art; open Wed–Sun 10am–6pm, Tues 2–6pm; admission
fee), Portugal's largest museum. It is housed on the site of
a Carmelite convent in a large and handsomely designed
palace on Rua das Janelas Verdes. On three floors, the
museum is an absorbing
place with at least several
masterpieces of interna-
tional renown.

> ### 'Nastiest city'
>
> Henry Fielding's *Journal of
> a Voyage to Lisbon*, published
> just after his death, ends
> with his arrival at seven in
> the evening: 'I got into a
> chaise on shore, and was
> driven through the nastiest
> city in the world…'

The ground floor (Piso 1)
has textiles and furniture
with a whole glittering salon,
plus paintings by foreign
artists, including Tiepolo,
Fragonard and, most strik-

The Temptation of St Anthony by Hieronymus Bosch

ingly, the Spaniard Francisco de Zurbarán, whose six larger-than-life saints once belonged to the monastery of São Vicente de Fora *(see page 29)*.

The same floor also has a triptych by Hieronymus Bosch – the Flemish artist who painted surreal allegorical scenes with alien-like creatures – that is both entertaining and horrific. *The Temptation of St Anthony*, painted around 1500, is a fantastic hallucination, tempered with humour and executed with mad genius. A crane rigged up like a helicopter, flying fish taxis and horse-size rats fill this ghoulish nightmare.

The second floor contains oriental art, much of it dating from the discoveries of the 15th and 16th centuries. Two Japanese lacquer screens depict the moment that the Portuguese – the first Europeans – landed in Japan. The new arrivals are depicted as villains up to no good, while the locals watch, amused, from their balconies. Also on this floor is silverware, mostly ecclesiastical.

The top floor is devoted to Portuguese art and sculpture. Here a highlight is *The Adoration of St Vincent,* a multi-panel work also taken from São Vicente de Fora monastery and attributed to the 15th-century Portuguese master, Nuno Gonçalves. It is a spectacular portrait of contemporary dignitaries, including Henry the Navigator. Dozens of others are shown in every range of *distracção* – ire, boredom and amusement – while several of the assembled clergymen appear as ugly, evil or both.

There is a pleasant garden and café, Café d'Arte, and the museum looks out over the **Doca do Alcântara**, where the **Fragata D. Fernando II e Glória** is berthed (open Tues–Sun 10am–5pm; admission fee). This beautiful vessel, the Portuguese navy's last sailing ship, was built in the Indian colony of Damão in 1843. The dock's brightly painted **Estação Maritima de Alcântara**, with murals by José Almada Negreiros, is where cruise-ship passengers come ashore. There are a number of bars and clubs in the terminal and around the dock, where there are also a couple of floating restaurants. The quay of the smaller **Doca de Santo Amaro** yachting marina, just beneath Ponte 25 de April, is lined with restaurants.

Custard tarts

The Belém district is famous for its special pastries (*pasteis de Belém*) – custard tarts coated with icing sugar and cinnamon. The highest-quality ones are generally regarded to be those sold at the Antigua Casa de Pastéis de Belém at Rua de Belém No. 84–88.

BELÉM

Belém (Portuguese for Bethlehem), Lisbon's primary monumental district, is a suburb about 6km (4 miles) west of Praça do Comércio. Land reclaimed from the river has been fashioned into parkland and marinas. Though the shore is unrecognisable today, the great Portuguese voyages of discovery in the 15th and 16th centuries set out from here.

Tram 15 makes the waterfront trip to Belém from Praça do Comércio; bus 201 from Cais do Sodré (just west of Praça do Comércio) covers virtually the same route but ends up at Linda-a-Velha.

Start a visit to Belém at the edge closest to central Lisbon. The **Museu Nacional dos Coches** (National Coach Museum; open Tues–Sun 10am–6pm; admission fee) is housed in the former riding school of the Belém Royal Palace. Two grand halls display dozens of

Museu Nacional dos Coches

impressive carriages, drawn by royal horses for ceremonial occasions both in the city and across the country over four centuries. The most extravagant are three sculpted, gilt carriages used by the Portuguese embassy in Rome in the early 18th century.

Mosteiro dos Jerónimos

Only a short stroll westwards along the Rua de Belém is Lisbon's largest and most impressive religious monument, the **Mosteiro dos Jerónimos** (Jerónimos Monastery), a UNESCO World Heritage Site. Commissioned by Manuel I with the windfall of riches brought back by Portuguese ships from the East, the monastery is an obvious testament to a

Mosteiro dos Jerónimos

confident and faithful nation. The convent wing was destroyed in the 1755 earthquake, but the church and cloister survive, classic examples of 16th-century style.

The vast south façade of the church, parallel to the river, is mostly unadorned limestone, making the few embellishments all the more remarkable. The main portal is a brilliant example of intricately carved stonework, as are the church's tall Manueline columns (this style bridged the gap between the Gothic and Renaissance styles in Portugal). The effect is one of immense height and space. The first architect in charge was a Frenchman, Diogo Boitac, who was succeeded by the Spaniard Juan de Castillo, responsible for the cloister and main portal.

Inside the church are the royal tombs of Manuel I, his wife Dona Maria, and others, set on pompous sculptured elephants, a tribute to the newly discovered marvels of the East. Near the west door are the modern tombs of two giants of Portugal's Golden Age, Vasco da Gama and the poet Luís de Camões.

Once you leave the church (don't miss the fine sculptural work surrounding the exterior of the main door), turn right and visit the **cloister** (open Tues–Sun 10am–5pm; admission fee), an airy two-level structure of strikingly original proportions and perspectives. Note the clever intersection of both sharp angles and arches. No two columns are the same.

The south section of the monastery has been largely restored and now houses the **Museu Nacional de Arqueologia** (National Museum of Archaeology; open Wed–Sun 10am–6pm, Tues 2–6pm; admission fee), an important collection of ancient relics, including Stone Age tools, Bronze Age jewels and,

Manueline Architecture

The Portuguese may be principally known for *azulejo* designs and port wine, but equally important is the ornate style of architecture and stone carving that suddenly appeared in Portugal in the late 15th century. It flourished for only a few decades, mostly during the reign of Manuel I (1495–1521), for which it was christened Manueline.

Probably triggered by the great ocean voyages of discovery, it took late Gothic as a base and added fanciful decoration, dramatic touches that were frequently references to the sea. Stone was carved like knotted rope and sculpted into imitation coral, seahorses, nets and waves, as well as non-nautical designs. The style first appeared in the small Igreja de Jesus in Setúbal, Lisbon's Torre de Belém and the Mosteiro dos Jerónimos. The style reached a peak of complexity in the unfinished chapels of the monastery at Batalha, between Lisbon and Coimbra. In the early 16th century, the style fell out of favour, and by 1540 Portugal had joined the rest of Europe in building in the more sober Renaissance style.

from Roman times, excellent sculptures and mosaics. The educational attractions continue just to the west of the monastery with a **Planetário** (Planetarium).

Portugal's fascinating maritime heritage is documented at the **Museu da Marinha** (Naval Museum; open Tues–Sun 10am–7pm, 6pm in winter; admission fee), which is housed in the west and northern wings of the monastery and in new buildings around the square opposite the entrance. Among the museum's collection are hundreds of models of various ship types down the ages, and numerous artefacts such as naval uniforms, maps and navigation equipment. Also on display is a delightful sculpture of the archangel Raphael that accompanied Vasco da Gama on his first voyage of exploration in 1497. Of more recent date are the handsome royal suites from *Amália*, the 1901 royal yacht that belonged to King Carlos I, who was an amateur marine biologist. Pride of place goes to the huge galliot, or brigantine, built in 1785 to celebrate a royal marriage, with seats for 80 oarsmen. The last time it was on the River Tagus was in 1957, carrying Queen Elizabeth II of Britain on a state visit. Next to it is the seaplane piloted by Portuguese aviators that in 1922 made the first flight across the South Atlantic.

Padrão dos Descobrimentos

The arresting **Padrão dos Descobrimentos** (Monument to the Discoveries; open Tues–Sun 10am–7pm, until 6pm in winter; admission fee), built in 1960 to commemorate the 500th anniversary of Henry the Navigator's death, juts

Padrão dos Descobrimentos

from the riverbank like a caravel cresting a wave. On the prow stands Prince Henry, looking out across the river and wearing, as always, his distinctive round hat. The figures behind him represent noted explorers, astronomers, map-makers, chroniclers and others instrumental in Portugal's Age of Discovery. A lift followed by stairs leads to the top and a superb view; the Lisbon Experience inside offers an audio-visual show.

Torre de Belém

Finally, there is the **Torre de Belém** (Tower of Belém; open Tues–Sun 10am–5pm; admission fee), erected in 1515 to def-end the entry to Lisbon. This fortress is one of the finest examples of Manueline architecture, with its battlements, cor-ner turrets and repeated theme of the Cross in the stonework. After crossing the wooden bridge, climb several floors to a top-level terrace that looks out over the Tagus. Though the much-

Torre de Belém

photographed monument may be smaller than you imagined, it must have been a wonderful sight to weary explorers returning from their journeys.

While you're at this end of town, don't miss the former royal residence, **Palácio da Ajuda** (open Thur–Tues 10am–5pm; admission fee), the biggest palace inside the city limits, which brims with all kinds of artworks and curiosities. Work began in 1802 to replace the temporary wooden palace erected here after the earthquake, but the royal family soon afterwards left for Brazil, and work was not continued again until the reign of Luís I (1861–89) and his Italian bride, Princess Maria Pia of Savoy, who became the first royals to live here. They furnished the palace with lavish trappings, including Gobelin tapestries, oriental ceramics and rare Portuguese furniture. The palace, which still has a rather unfinished air, is north of Belém up Calçada da Ajuda.

NORTH LISBON

At the north end of Avenida da Liberdade, beyond the Marquês de Pombal rotunda, is a formal park, **Parque Eduardo VII**. The well-manicured lawns and shrubs are surrounded on either side by wooded areas and gardens. So thrilled were the Portuguese by a royal visit at the turn of the last century that they named the park after Britain's king, Edward VII.

Estufa Fria

Lisbon's most original botanical triumph occupies the north-west corner of the park. Known as **Estufa Fria** (the Cold House; open 9am–4.30pm), this garden was created in the early 20th century on the site of a quarry, and it owes its name to the fact that its simple wooden lath roof gives shade but no heat, allowing plants from a variety of backgrounds to grow as naturally as possible, protected from the Lisboan extremes of climate. Paths weave their way through the enormous space among species from Africa, Asia and South America. At the far side, a doorway leads through to the cavernous **Estufa Quente** (the Hot House), which was built at the end of the 1950s on the highest point of the quarry. Its roof and walls are made of glass, in order to capture the maximum amount of light and heat, and hence more tropical species thrive here.

Inside the Estufa Quente

Museu Gulbenkian

To the north of Parque Eduardo VII, off Avenida António Augusto Aguiar, at Avenida da Berna 45, is Lisbon's most remarkable museum, **Museu Gulbenkian** (Gulbenkian Museum; open Tues–Sun 10am–6pm; admission fee). It was created to house one of the finest private art collections in Europe, acquired by an

Armenian billionaire, Calouste Gulbenkian, and later bequeathed to the Portuguese state. A great philanthropist who died in Lisbon in 1955, Gulbenkian meticulously acquired acclaimed masterpieces and built up an excellent and wide-ranging collection.

Surrounded by its own perfectly planned and maintained park, built at a time when concrete was on the cutting edge of architecture, the huge collection begins chronologically, with Egyptian ceramics and sculptures dating back to around 2700BC, delicate and perfectly preserved. The handsome statue of the judge Bes is inscribed with hieroglyphs that date it from the reign of Pharaoh Psamtik I (7th century BC).

Calouste Gulbenkian

At the dawn of the Oil Age, a far-sighted Turkish-born Armenian put up money to help finance drilling in Mesopotamia (now Iraq), then part of the Turkish empire. For his part, he received 5 percent of the Iraq Petroleum Company. Two world wars and the fuelling of millions of cars, planes and ships made Calouste Gulbenkian rich beyond imagination. He became a knowledgeable and dedicated collector of antiquities and great art, beginning with Turkish and Persian carpets, Armenian and Arabic manuscripts, and Greek and Roman coins. His passions spread to include ancient Egyptian art, Chinese porcelain and Western painting. His mission was acquiring perfect examples in each of his chosen fields.

Gulbenkian (who had British nationality for much of his life) was preparing to travel to the United States when he fell ill in Lisbon. He was so impressed with his treatment here that he decided to stay, establishing a philanthropic foundation to which he left most of his money and his collections when he died in 1955. The Gulbenkian Museum is his centrepiece, complemented by several other cultural facilities in Portugal, including the Modern Art Centre, regional museums, a planetarium and educational institutes.

A large section of the museum is devoted to art of the Islamic East, and includes ancient fabrics, costumes and carpets, plus ceramics, glassware and illuminated pages from the Koran. The survey of Western art begins in the 11th century with illuminated parchment manuscripts. Tiny ivory sculptures of religious scenes come from 14th-century France, and there are a number of well-preserved tapestries from the Flemish and Italian workshops of the 16th century.

Rembrandt's *Figure of an Old Man*, Gulbenkian Museum

Paintings by Dutch and Flemish masters include works by Hals, Van Dyck and Ruysdael. Pride of place is given to two Rembrandts: the sensitive portrait *Figure of an Old Man* and a painting of a helmeted warrior believed to be Pallas Athene or Alexander the Great, probably modelled by Rembrandt's son Titus.

The impressive hall of Chinese porcelain begins with the Yuan dynasty (13th–14th century; around the time of Marco Polo) and goes on to some exquisite items from the 17th and 18th centuries. Miraculously unmarred by the forces of time, each object is representative of the pinnacle of a particular school of art.

The last room of the museum contains 169 items by Gulbenkian's friend René Lalique (1860–1945), the talented and versatile French jeweller. On display are Art Nouveau pendants, bracelets, necklaces, brooches and combs of assorted materials and unexpected motifs.

The **Centro de Arte Moderna** (open Tues–Fri 10am–6pm; a combined ticket with the main museum can be bought) is also a part of the Gulbenkian Foundation. This is the best place to see 20th-century Portuguese art, and there are some excellent works by Amadeo de Souza Cardoso and Almada Negreiros, particularly of society types and Lisbon café life. There are also a couple of early Paula Rego abstracts, from 1935. The Foundation runs exhibition and concert halls where musical performances and ballets take place. There is also a library, with occasional free lunchtime Sunday concerts, a bookshop and a restaurant.

Aqueduto das Águas Livres

A landmark that is most often seen by those heading out of town is the soaring arches of **Aqueduto das Águas Livres** (a freshwater aqueduct), which spans an impressive 18km (11 miles) across the Alcântara valley north of downtown Lisbon. Fresh water was first carried across the aqueduct in 1748; it managed to survive the earthquake, and water is carried across it still. A visit to the aqueduct can be arranged through the **Museu de Água** (Water Museum; open Mon–Sat 10am–6pm; admission fee) in the city's first steam-pumping station, in Rua do Alviela near Santa Apolónia station. However, for the most

Aqueduto das Águas Livres

impressive views from underneath, it's best to avoid the museum and walk down the road.

Along with the motorway to Cascais, the aqueduct slices through the city's biggest park, **Monsanto**. Eucalyptus, cypress, cedar, umbrella pines and oak trees all thrive on the rolling hillsides. Apart from calm and fresh air, the park contains sports grounds, bars and restaurants. Its municipal camping ground ranks as one of Europe's prettiest and best-organised, and the park also has some impressive *miradouros*, giving outstanding views over Lisbon and the estuary. Be warned, though, that its roads usually turn into a traffic jam at rush hours.

PARQUE DAS NAÇÕES

Lisbon, and the whole of Portugal, pinned much hope on the city's hosting of the World Expo in 1998. Celebrating the 'Heritage of the Oceans', it was an opportunity for the nation to pay tribute to its former maritime greatness and reintroduce itself to the world.

Park panorama

A high point of the Parque das Nações is the 145m (475ft) Torre Vasco da Gama with a panoramic terrace and restaurant in the 'crow's nest' 104m (341ft) above ground.

Lisbon used the occasion to reinvigorate a run-down industrial area east of the city, creating a high-tech entertainment park, along with new shopping and nightlife areas. A futuristic railway station, **Estação do Oriente** (designed by the Spanish architect Santiago Calatrava as a major terminal for destinations around the country), a pristine shopping mall and the stark white Vasco da Gama bridge extending across the Tagus into the horizon – Europe's longest bridge at 17.2km (10¾ miles) – frame the park.

Oceanário de Lisboa

The **Parque das Nações** (Nations' Park) complex extends 5km (3 miles) along the riverfront, principally drawing visitors to its world-class aquarium, which served as the Oceans Pavilion during the Expo, and has since become one of the city's primary attractions. The complex won the award for best urban development in Iberia in 1999. Designed by the American Peter Chermayeff, the **Oceanário de Lisboa** (open daily 10am–7pm, 6pm in winter; admission fee), which looks something like a marooned oil derrick or space station from the set of a sci-fi thriller, is one of the largest and finest aquariums in the world. It houses large tanks representing different oceans (Antarctic, Indian, Pacific and Atlantic), with more than 10,000 examples of marine life and 200 species taken from across the world. As visitors make their way around the massive circular aquarium – the size of four Olympic-size swimming pools – tiger sharks, manta rays and schools of brightly coloured fish glide silently by, overhead and underneath observation decks.

Nations' Park is a good place for families, even though it can be devoid of life during the week. There are whimsical fountains, paddle boats, garden playgrounds, bowling lanes,

A spectacular aquarium – Oceanário de Lisboa

Atlântico Hall arena, with modern housing in the background

aerial cable cars running the length of the waterfront, and the **Torre Vasco da Gama**, a tower with an observation deck – the tallest structure in Portugal – that looks out to the Atlantic and back down the river at Lisbon. The **Pavilhão do Conhecimento** (the Pavilion of Knowledge; open Tues–Fri 10am–6pm, Sat–Sun 11am–7pm; admission fee), is a museum of science and technology with a cyber café.

Sporting events, such as basketball and tennis, and concerts by big-name international performers as well as top locals, are held at the mushroom-like **Atlântico Hall** arena, which functioned as the Utopia Pavilion during the Expo. The **Teatro Camões** is home to the excellent national ballet company.

Many restaurants and bars have moved into the marina area, transforming it into an animated nightspot; hotels and residential housing are being built, creating a desirable suburb, and the mall around the Metro station attracts late-night and Sunday shoppers.

Among the former pavilions notable for their architectural interest is the **Portugal Pavilion** beside the marina, by the Pritzker prize-winning Portuguese architect Álvaro Siza Vieira. The pavilion has an astonishing curved and suspended roof 67m (221ft) long and weighing 1,400 tonnes.

ACROSS THE TAGUS

With a span of 2.3km (1½ miles), the **Ponte 25 de Abril** across the River Tagus became the longest suspension bridge in Europe when it was opened in 1966. Originally named in honour of the nation's dictator, after the revolution of 1974 the name 'Salazar' was removed, and for quite a time it was known simply as 'the bridge'. In an about-face, it was renamed after the date of the Carnation Revolution, 25 April. In 1999 a sixth lane was added to it, and a railway line was suspended beneath it. Though its bold red colour is quite striking, the bridge lacks the grace of the Golden Gate Bridge in San Francisco with which it is often compared.

Just across the river, above Cacilhas and looming up over the bridge's tollbooths, is Lisbon's take on Rio de Janeiro's landmark, the **statue of Cristo Rei** (Christ the King). Almost 30m (100ft) tall, it stands on a pedestal that is another 82m (269ft) high. A chapel, the Santuário de Cristo Rei, is housed in the base of the monument, where there is also a cafeteria. Take the lift up to the viewing terrace at the top of the pedestal for a glorious 360-degree panorama of the estuary, the bridge, all of Lisbon and a vast expanse of Portugal to the south, including the Serra da Arrábida (see page 76).

Visiting the statue

To visit the statue of Cristo Rei you can drive across the bridge or take one of the orange ferries from Cais do Sodré to Cacilhas and then a taxi or a bus marked 'Cristo Rei'.

EXCURSIONS FROM LISBON

One of the great attractions of Lisbon is the number of desirable excursions only a very short distance from the capital – there are highlights west, south and north of the city. Whether you're looking for grand palaces, beach resorts, awe-inspiring abbeys or a charming romantic town lodged in the mountains, there's plenty to explore in the environs.

Queluz

An easy half-day outing is to **Palácio Nacional de Queluz** (open Wed–Mon 9.30am–5pm; admission fee), 14km (9 miles) west of Lisbon. To reach it, take a bus tour or a commuter train from Rossio station to Queluz-Belas. By car it's 20 minutes on the motorway through the forest of Monsanto; the turn-off on the way to Sintra is clearly signposted. You're hardly out of Lisbon's mushrooming suburbs before you're alongside the elegant palace.

Pedro III commissioned this sumptuous, pretty pink summer palace, which was built in the second half of the 18th century by the Frenchman Jean-Baptiste Robillon and the Portuguese Mateus Vicente de Oliveira. As a working official residence for the royal family, Queluz thrived mostly during the reign of Maria I (1777–99), Pedro III's wife. The queen suffered from bouts of depression, which deepened into madness, and visitors to the palace told of her shrieking fits.

Closed on Tuesdays

Most museums in Portugal are closed on Monday, but Queluz takes Tuesday off – and any other day when visiting heads of state are in residence.

From the road, the palace seems relatively unprepossessing, but inside, Portuguese modesty is totally abandoned, and Queluz is a model of only slightly tattered splendour. Though the palace lost much to French invasions (it was used by General Andoche Junot as his headquarters during the Peninsular War) and a 1934 fire, it manages to preserve an air of 18th-century royal privilege. The **throne room** is one of the most lavish, with overpowering chandeliers and walls and ceilings layered with gilt. The **Sala dos Embaixadores** (Hall of Ambassadors) has a floor like a huge chessboard in addition to a wealth of mirrors and a *trompe l'oeil* ceiling. Queluz is rather curiously laid out – public rooms almost incoherently border living quarters.

The **Palace Gardens** are the pride of Queluz and are never-ending, with clipped hedges in perfect geometric array, bushes barbered into inventive shapes, imaginative fountains and armies of statues. The huge old magnolia trees and orange trees close by relieve some of the formality. Royal guests once entered the garden via the pompous but original **Escadaria**

Palácio Nacional de Queluz

By train to Sintra

Sintra's one-lane entry road is jammed with waiting cars and tourist buses from 8am to 6pm. It's advisable to take the train from Lisbon so you don't have to worry about parking.

dos Leões (Lions' Staircase). In the early 19th century dozens of live animals – not just dogs, but lions and wolves – were boarded at Queluz, which was then the site of the royal zoo.

Queluz has one rather original attraction, a man-made river. Enclosed between retaining walls covered in precious *azulejos*, a real stream was diverted to pass through the huge palace grounds, and was dammed so that the level of the water could be raised whenever the royal residents wanted to go for a boat ride.

The former royal kitchen has been converted into a prestigious restaurant run by the *pousada* hotel chain. With giant old utensils, a fireplace big enough for a crowd to walk into, and lots of atmosphere, the place is called – understandably – *Cozinha Velha,* or 'Old Kitchen'.

Sintra

Though **Sintra** suffers the effects of its enduring popularity, it is one of the finest towns in Portugal to visit, and is easily reached by train from Rossio. Nestled into the Serra de Sintra, 25km (16 miles) northwest of Lisbon, it was once a coveted summer retreat for royals; today it's a romantic getaway for people from all over the world. Clustered throughout the forested hillsides are old palaces and estates with spectacular vistas. Two peaks in the range are crowned by reminders of Sintra's illustrious past: Castelo dos Mouros, the ruins of a castle built by occupying Moors in the 8th century, and Palácio de Pena, the multicoloured fantasy palace built by a German nobleman for his Portuguese wife. The views from either of these points extends as far as the sea, and the entire area, thick with vegetation and paths through the hills, is spectacular for trekkers.

Right in the centre of town is the **Palácio Nacional de Sintra** (also called the *Paço Real*, or Royal Palace; open Thur–Tues 10am–1pm; admission fee). Except for its two huge, white conical chimneys, from the outside it looks like a fairly ordinary hulk of a palace. Its real treasures lie inside. A summer home for Portuguese kings since the early 14th century, the palace's design became more and more unpredictable and haphazard as wings were added over the centuries, with back-to-back medieval and Manueline styles. The resulting interiors and furnishings are remarkable, including some of the oldest and most valuable *azulejos* in Portugal.

Every room in the Palácio Nacional has a story to tell. During the 17th century, the dull-witted Afonso VI was pressured into abdicating for the benefit of the country, therefore

The Palácio Nacional de Sintra, with its distinctive chimneys

Castelo dos Mouros
from far below Sintra

allowing his more effective brother, Pedro II, to become king. When a plot to restore Afonso to the throne was discovered, the former monarch was exiled to Sintra. For nine years, until he died in 1683, he was imprisoned in a simple room of the Palácio Nacional. It's said that the worn floor is a result of Afonso's constant pacing up and down.

A large ground-floor hall, **Sala das Pegas** (Magpie Salon), tells a very different story. João I (1385–1433) was caught by Queen Philippa kissing one of her ladies-in-waiting. The palace gossips had a field day until the king ordered the entire ceiling of the hall closed and painted with magpies, as many as there were ladies-in-waiting, their mouths sealed. The royal rebuke, the king's way of saying 'so what' and 'shut up', had the desired effect.

The so-called **Sala dos Cisnes** (Swan Room) is decorated with ceiling panels painted with swans, each in a different position. There are also ceilings with intricate designs in the *mudéjar* style influenced by Moorish art.

The palace's landmark chimneys, shaped like inverted cones, were used to let the smoke out of the massive kitchen when oxen were being roasted for large banquets given for visiting dignitaries.

Castelo dos Mouros

A special bus climbs a steep road with hairpin turns into the *serra* from Sintra to visit some spectacular monuments. The oldest, **Castelo dos Mouros** (Moors' Castle; open 9am–7pm; admission fee), hugs a rocky ridge overlooking the town. It was erected during the 8th century, soon after the Moors occupied Portugal. The dauntless Afonso Henriques conquered it for the Christians in 1147, a major victory in the reconquest of Portugal. Today the castle is a ruin, but a fascinating one, its crenellated walls still severe. Those with the energy to do so should climb the ramparts to the top for incredible views of the entire forested area all the way out to sea and across the treetops to Sintra's most famous monument, the Palácio da Pena. It's easy to pick out individual *quintas* (estates) in their privileged seclusion.

Palácio da Pena

Farther up the same winding road on the hilltop, the **Palácio da Pena** (open Tues–Sat 10am–7pm, 6pm in winter; admission fee), more than 450m (1,500ft) above sea-level, is an outrageous Victorian folly reached by way of a park so lush with flowering trees and vines it resembles a tropical

Sintra's Country Market

On the second and last Sunday of each month, a country fair is held in São Pedro do Sintra, a village adjacent to Sintra – be prepared to encounter traffic jams. In the open market you can buy home-made bread, cheese and sausages, or even a bottle of patent medicine sold to you by an old-fashioned, slick-talking hawker. Antiques collectors will find many possibilities here, including religious statues and rustic furniture, as well as ordinary 19th-century household appliances. The major annual fair is held here on 29 June.

The extravagant Palácio da Pena

rainforest. In 1511, Manuel I had a monastery built on this site. It was mostly destroyed in the earthquake of 1755, though a notable chapel and cloister survive. The present building is a bizarre and extravagant cocktail of Gothic, Renaissance, Manueline and Moorish architecture, fashioned as a love nest for Maria II (1834–53) and her smitten husband, Ferdinand of Saxe-Coburg-Gotha. Few have had the wealth to indulge their free-running fantasies so grandly. Like a child's dream castle, the exterior is a wild, layered construction painted pink, yellow, grey and red, with crenellated turrets, a studded archway and monsters guarding doorways. Inside, rooms are full of imaginative, ornate and, in some cases, suffocatingly sumptuous details. The views from the Disney-esque terraces of the platforms sweep all the way from the Atlantic to Lisbon.

Also located in and around Sintra are: the **Quinta da Regaleira**, a fantastic late 19th-century turreted mansion;

the **Montserrate Palace Gardens**, wild, lush, and ideal for hiking; the **Palácio de Seteais**, an 18th-century palace, today Sintra's fanciest hotel; the **Museu do Brinquedo**, a 20,000-piece toy museum; and Sintra's excellent **Museum of Modern Art**. A short hop from Sintra are the attractive village of **Colares** and the beach at **Praia das Maçãs**. Sintra's helpful tourist information office, on Praça da República in the old quarter, can direct you to any of these.

Mafra

The **Palácio Nacional de Mafra** (open Tues–Sun 10am–4.30pm; admission fee) is 40km (25 miles) to the northwest of Lisbon, and can be reached by bus from Campo Grande. In modest Portugal, the dimensions of this convent and palace are really quite staggering. The frontage of the building, often likened to Spain's Escorial, measures over 220m (726ft). Mafra is so enormous that it is clearly visible from Sintra, approximately 16km (10 miles) away.

This monumental extravagance is attributable to João V, who in 1711 conceived this project to celebrate the long-awaited birth of his first child, Princess Dona Maria, after three years of marriage. A few statistics show the colossal scale of the project: 5,200 doorways, 2,500 windows and a 50,000-strong army of artists, artisans and labourers. A single carillon of 50 bells cost a shipload of gold. 'So cheap?' the king is said to have exclaimed. 'I'll take two.'

Inside Mafra's church

The free guided tour of the monastery-palace lasts

about an hour, and takes you from the apartments of João V at one end of the structure to the queen's apartments at the other end. The convent **library** is the undisputed highlight; it has a vaulted ceiling, a precious wood floor and tall shelves housing 30,000 books, making it the largest one-room library in Portugal. The **hospital** is a church with 16 private sickrooms lining the nave, so that patients could hear mass from their beds.

At Mafra is the church of Santo André, where Pedro Hispano was a priest before becoming Pope John XI in 1276, He remains Portugal's only pope.

Ericeira

Another 10km (6 miles) towards the coast is the fishing village and growing resort of **Ericeira**. The old section is a winsome town of cobbled streets winding between white-

Whitewashed Ericeira

washed cottages, with everything clean, neat and treasured by inhabitants and visitors alike.

Ericeira received its town charter around 750 years ago, but scarcely attracted any attention until 1910, when Portugal's last king, Manuel II, hastily arrived from Mafra, and in its little port, boarded the royal yacht with his family to sail off into exile.

Filleting fish at Ericeira

Estoril Coast

The Costa do Estoril (formerly called Costa do Sol) begins just west of Lisbon and goes all the way around the tip of the peninsula to Guincho on the open Atlantic. Those seeking pollution-free swimming *(see page 90)* usually head for Guincho, but the famous old resort of Estoril itself, some 24km (15 miles) from Lisbon, is still worth a visit.

The half-hour train journey from Cais do Sodré station in Lisbon to Estoril goes through former fishing villages now turned into soulless commuter suburbs. If you go by the motorway (toll road) you will see nothing of them at all, but the coastal road still provides a scenic drive.

The railway station at **Estoril** is right alongside the beach. On the other side of the tracks (and across the coast road) is a formal park, the front lawn of the town's glitzy **casino**. With its nightclub, restaurants, bars, cinema, exhibition halls, shops and gaming rooms, this is Estoril's one-stop, after-dark amusement centre. In spite of the modern decor, the casino maintains an old-fashioned pace. Gambling is

Elegant hotel at Cascais

suspended only two nights a year: Good Friday and Christmas Eve. Legend has it that somebody broke the bank one Good Friday, prompting a superstitious management to declare it a holiday thenceforth. (Officials dismiss the story as wishful thinking.)

The rest of Estoril is about as discreet as a Las Vegas high roller. Victorian villas and sleek modern mansions are tucked away behind green curtains of palms, eucalyptus, pines and vines. In the first half of the 20th century, dignitaries and monarchs, either unexpectedly unemployed or exiled, gravitated to Estoril or Cascais and luxurious hideaways.

As early as the mid-18th century, Estoril was attracting visitors because of its balmy climate and thermal spa baths, which were considered good for liver complaints. Long before that, however, prehistoric settlers had built cave-cemeteries, discovered in 1944 near the beach, dug out of the limestone.

Cascais

While Estoril is a full-scale resort – cosmopolitan and sybaritic – **Cascais**, which sits on a pretty curved bay, lives a double life. It is a town of both fishermen and kings, where the humble and the retiring rich coexist with camera-toting visitors. The workaday fishing scene attracts tourists, who inspect the catch as it is unloaded from boats into wooden trays and then rushed to the modern auction building. There the fish are sold by a reverse (Dutch) auction, in which the price starts high and decreases until somebody shouts a bid. You may not understand the auctioneer's chant, but you'll see what he's selling: lobster, shrimp, hake, squid and sardines. Retail sales are in the hands of local fishwives, who set up stalls outside the market. For the finished product, try any of the dozen restaurants within walking distance of the beach.

The main square is a charmer. The **Paços do Concelho** (Town Hall) has stately windows with iron railings, separated by panels of *azulejos* depicting saints. The fire station occupies a place of honour between the town hall and an attractive church, while in the main square, with undulating designs in its mosaic pavement, stands a statue of Pedro I.

The sturdy-looking 17th-century fort, the **Cidadela** (Citadel), now occupied by the military, is one of the few buildings to have survived the earthquake and tidal wave of 1755. A chapel within the walls contains an image of St Anthony, traditionally carried on the back of a white mule in the parade on the feast day of Santo António (13 June).

Paços do Concelho, Cascais

After an overdose of sun and salt, the municipal park down the road is a cool relief. The palace in this park is a lovely villa housing the **Museu dos Condes de Castro Guimarães** (Museum of the Counts of Castro Guimarães; open Tues–Sun 10am–5pm; admission fee), a museum with archeological remains, artworks, old furniture, gold and silver. For a more complete picture of the resort's fishing heritage and royal connections, visit the intriguing **Museu do Mar – Rei Dom Carlos** (King Carlos Museum of the Seas; open Tues–Sun 10am–5pm; admission fee), which has historic photographs of the king, who was an enthusiastic marine biologist, at leisure, as well as the costumes and customs of the fisherfolk.

The road out of Cascais to the west passes **Boca do Inferno** (Mouth of Hell), a geological curiosity where, in rough weather, the waves send up astonishingly high spouts

Cascais and its beachfront

of spray accompanied by ferocious sound effects. On a day when the sea is calm, you'll wonder what all the fuss is about.

Cabo da Roca

At **Guincho**, you have the choice of either a sandy beach or the rocks to fish from, but be careful – they face the open sea and it's often rough, and hence a windsurfer's heaven. Just up the coast you can see the windswept cape of **Cabo da**

Cabo da Roca

Roca, the most westerly point of mainland Europe. You can reach the cape by continuing on from Guincho, through Malveira, and then turning left. A right turn at the same points leads you along a winding road through the glorious, pine-scented **Serra de Sintra**, finishing up back in Sintra *(see page 64)*.

South of Lisbon

Sesimbra

It's around 32km (20 miles) south from Lisbon over the bridge to the calm, clean seashore at **Sesimbra**. The beach, the main draw for the mostly Portuguese crowd that gathers here at weekends and holidays, not least for its splendid seafood restaurants, is narrow but long, and is sheltered from the brunt of Atlantic tides and harsh winds. Sesimbra is an important fishing centre, and most of the local adult male population seems to be involved in the industry. Fishing boats set out from the **harbour** at the far, western end of the town,

Sesimbra viewed from its castle

to bring home their catches of sardine and horse mackerel, hake and swordfish.

Largo 5 de Outubro is a small square in the centre of town, where locals sit and gossip under a giant floral canopy of bougainvillea. Adjacent is the **Misericórdia Church**, with its upturned keel roof. Founded during the 15th century, it contains the much venerated image of Senhor Jesus das Chagas, the patron of the Sesimbra fishing community.

Those **castle walls** silhouetted on the hilltop above Sesimbra are the genuine article, though recently restored. During the Middle Ages the whole town was situated up there, protected against sea raiders by the walls and the altitude. The Moors built the enclave, lost it to Dom Afonso Henriques in 1165, and won it back again for a few years before having to move out permanently in 1200. Inside the outer fortifications is the Church of Our Lady of the Consolation of the Castle, destroyed during the 12th century and rebuilt during the 18th. It's well worth taking a peek inside: the walls are covered in *azulejos* from floor to ceiling. The castle is open daily and free to visitors. The view down to the curve of the coast and back to the Arrábida mountains is magnificent.

Serra da Arrábida

The topographical highlight of the Arrábida peninsula is the **Serra da Arrábida**, a mountain chain approximately

35km (22 miles) long that protects the coast from the strong north winds and accounts for the Mediterranean vegetation. In the west the peninsula ends with the dramatic cliffs of **Cabo Espichel**. The 12km (7½-mile) route across the Serra is winding and narrow, but it provides an attractive introduction to the wonderfully rugged **Parque Natural da Arrábida**, which covers more than 10,000 hectares (24,700 acres). From the depths of the sea the Serra rises a sheer 500m (1,650ft). Science describes this rolling heathland as a glacial relict, its primitive forests preserved when glaciers melted. Wild slopes contrast with the intense blue of the sea below; come in spring and the park is bright with wild flowers. The old monastery nestled in the hills has been resurrected as part of Lisbon University. Down below, on the coast, the little beach spot of **Portinho da Arrábida** is popular with Portuguese weekenders.

Vineyards with the Serra da Arrábida behind

Setúbal

Setúbal, the district capital, is a 20-minute drive from Lisbon by motorway, longer if you take the picturesque route via Sesimbra and Arrábida. (The bus does it in an hour; or you can take the ferry across the Tagus and then the slow local train, a total of an hour and a half.) This is olive and citrus country, with cows grazing among the trees. The farther south you go, the more significant the vineyards; the Setúbal region produces a highly regarded Muscatel.

Setúbal is a conglomeration of market town, industrial centre and resort, and is Portugal's third-largest fishing port. Narrow, inviting shopping streets twist through the centre of the city. Its greatest historical and artistic treasure, the Gothic **Igreja de Jesus**, was built around 1490 by the great French architect Boitac, who later built Lisbon's glorious Jerónimos Monastery *(see page 47)*. A dramatic main portal leads into the church, which boasts two inspired elements of decoration: 17th-century *azulejos* on the walls, and stone pillars like twisted strands of clay, fragile-looking in spite of their obviously solid dimensions.

The adjoining monastery has been converted into the **Museu de Cidade** (Town Museum; open Tues–Sun 9.30am–12.30pm, 2–5pm; admission fee), with a mixture of early Portuguese paintings, including a series of the life of Jesus, archaeological odds and ends, antique furniture and tiles. The cloister was reconstructed after the 1755 earthquake, but since then excavation has revealed parts of the original patio.

The 16th-century star-shaped fort, high above the town to the west, is now a government-sponsored *pousada* with great views *(see page 136)*. There's usually some action taking place down in the fishermen's quarter when brightly painted boats of all sizes return with freshly caught fish.

Fishing boats at Setúbal

WHAT TO DO

SHOPPING

Lisbon is a cosmopolitan city, but many of its shops show that it hasn't lost its old-fashioned sense of style or its traditional crafts. Here you can buy expensive and intricate works of gold and silver, or handicrafts that have been produced for hundreds of years. There are also chic boutiques, glittering malls and a wonderfully scruffy outdoor market.

Best Buys

Handicrafts excel in Portugal. **Azulejos**, the hand-painted ceramic tiles that have been decorating Portugal's walls throughout the centuries, are one of the top crafts. You can buy a scene on a single blue-and-white tile, an address plaque for your house or a batch to assemble into a picture when you get home. Some shops will paint tiles to order if you have a particular design in mind, and some will copy a photograph. Delicate Portuguese **embroidery** and **lacework**, especially samples by women on the island of Madeira, is excellent. Hand-embroidered goods also come from the Azores and some mainland towns, notably Viana do Castelo.

> ### Shopping Card
>
> The Lisboa Shopping Card offers discounts of up to 20 percent in Baixa, Chiado and Av. Liberdade. The card is available in 1- to 3-day versions from Turismo de Lisboa offices.

    Filigree work is of very high quality. Look for silver filigree earrings and brooches, often in the form of flowers or butterflies. Portuguese **pottery** and **ceramics** are found in

Fado performers

Luvaria Ulisses, on Rua do Carmo, sells fine gloves

many designs and colours, from fine porcelain **Vista Alegre** to folksy earthenware. Hand-painted brightly coloured **cockerels** from Barcelos have become a national symbol.

Arraiolos, an Alentejo village, has been making fine **wool rugs** in bright colours and graceful designs for centuries. **Hand-woven baskets**, which differ by region, are strong, utilitarian and often pretty. As a bonus, they can carry other purchases home. Artefacts made from **cork** are typical; Portugal is the world's leading producer, not only for wine bottles but even for umbrellas and bags.

Speaking of wine, Portugal has long been famous for its fortified **port wine** from the Douro Valley near Oporto in the north. Best known as an after-dinner tradition, it also comes in aperitif versions *(see pages 101–2)*. Vintage port of the most select years is what connoisseurs and collectors seek, but there are more accessible ports to take home. Look for aged tawnys, LBV (late bottle vintages) or, for something a little more unusual, a bottle of white port.

Madeira wine, from the volcanic soil of the Portuguese island in the Atlantic, is served either before dinner or afterwards as a dessert wine. While these regional wines get much of the attention, Portugal also produces a number of excellent red and white table wines, which make good gifts and souvenirs. Look for those from Dão and Alentejo, as well as *vinhos verdes* (young wines) from the Minho.

To enjoy the sounds of Portugal back home, take home a classic **fado recording**, perhaps by the late Amália Rodrigues or by Carlos Paredes, or a disc of ethereal Portuguese **pop** by the Lisbon group Madredeus.

Antiques collectors often browse in the shops in Rua Dom Pedro V, the bustling street descending from the Rato to Cais do Sodré, and Rua de São José in Graça, the district behind Alfama.

Much of the **clothing** you'll see in Lisbon comes from international chain stores, though a number of **high-fashion designers** from Portugal – such as Ana Salazar and Fátima Lopes – have gained international attention, and Chiado is a good place to seek them out. Hand-knitted pullovers in sophisticated designs or chunky fishermen's sweaters from Nazaré are good buys.

Inside Centro Columbo

Leather belts, bags and shoes are popular buys. Shoes are fashionable, and excellent value.

Where to Shop

Most city shops are open Monday to Friday from 9am to 1pm and from 3pm to 7pm; the more traditional shops close on Saturday at 1pm. Modern shopping malls are usually open from 10am to midnight or later, and sometimes on Sunday. Some of the Baixa shops stay open during lunchtime.

Wares for sale at the Feira da Ladra

Principal shopping areas include **Vasco da Gama** mall at Oriente, which is open until 10pm seven nights a week. **Avenida da Liberdade** has smart shops and, above it, in Rua Augusta with an entrance in São Sebastião Metro, is the seven-storey **Corte Inglés**. This stylish department store has excellent clothing departments, plus a good electronics section, lovely accessories, gloves and bags, as well as a large food section in the basement. There are cafés throughout the store if you need a rest.

The **Chiado** district is the place to go for books, smart designer wear and interiors, especially the **Armazéns do Chiado** mall and Rua Garrett. The French-owned Fnac department store here is popular.

The central grid of streets around Rua Augusta in the **Baixa** contains wonderfully atmospheric shops, sustained by low rents. Traditional foodstuffs, clothes and jewellery are all on sale here.

Across the street from Cais de Sodre station is the **Mercado da Ribeira**. The upper floor is now often used by the Lisbon Tourism and Cultural Centre. Here you can obtain genuine regional handicrafts and food products. Folk music and dance performances and exhibitions also take place. On Sundays, from 9am to 1pm, a collectors' market is held.

Markets are fun for their ambience as much as the goods for sale. Behind São Vicente de Fora church, in the Campo de Santa Clara, the **Feira da Ladra** ('Thieves' Market') is held on Tuesday and Saturday from dawn to dusk. On the fringes of the kitchenware and clothing stalls are dusty treasures and an incredible range of second-hand items.

Lisbon has two main shopping centres. **Amoreiras** (Avenida Engenheiro Duarte Pacheco) is a pastel-coloured complex laid out over three floors. It houses banks, a post office, cinemas, a health club, supermarkets, a chapel, art galleries, eating places and some 300 shops selling goods from furniture and linen to music, books, china and chocolate. **Centro Columbo** (Avenida Lusiada, Benfica; Metro: Colégio Militar) is the city's largest shopping centre, more akin to a massive leisure complex than a mere shopping mall. Come here for all the major chains, plus a nursery, chapel, cinema, health club, golf driving range, bowling alley and funfair.

Out near Cascais, beside the motorway, **Cascaisshopping** is another shopping complex. For easy shopping closer to town, you might like to try the **Centro Commercial de Alvalade** and the fashionable but generally expensive **Avenida da Roma**.

ENTERTAINMENT

The Portuguese capital has a wide variety of nightlife options, and hot new clubs and bars are springing up in the newly renovated areas along the River Tagus.

Nightclubs, Bars and Live Music. The classic night-time outing in Lisbon is still to the *fado* houses in Alfama or Bairro Alto. A century ago, 'respectable' people were reluctant to be seen in a *fado* club; nowadays the danger is not to your reputation, only to your wallet, as tickets are quite expensive. Many offer dinner as well as drinks. Inclusive tours are available.

In Bairro Alto you can also find conventional discos, nightclubs, jazz clubs and bars for all tastes, some open until 5am. Clubs to consider include: Adega Machado (Rua do Norte 91; tel: 213 224 640; Metro: Chiado); A Parreirinha da Alfama (Beco do Espírito Santo 1; tel: 218 868 209); Lisboa à Noite (Rua das Gáveas 69; tel: 213 462 603); Luso (Travessa da Queimada 10; tel: 213 422 281; Metro: Chiado); A Severa (lunchtime, Rua das Gáveas 51; tel: 213 428 314); and Senhor Vinho (Rua do Meio à Lapa 18; tel: 213 972 681; Metro: Avenida).

Fado

Fado, the soulful Portuguese song – literally 'fate', translated into music – is based on a story or poem and accompanied by a 12-string guitar. The dramatic atmosphere of a *fado* house adds to the occasion. Guitarists start off the proceedings with a warm-up number. The lights dim, the audience goes quiet, and a spotlight picks out a woman in black who begins to wail out a song of tragedy and despair. Her sultry voice sums up that most Portuguese emotion, *saudade* – a swell of longing, regret and nostalgia. Though most often characterised by melancholy or despair, there are also joyful and relatively upbeat *fados*.

Most *fado* singers are women, but you are also likely hear a man perform the same sort of ballad with a strong, husky voice. The *fado* is much too solemn to be danced. Instead, regional fishermen's and shepherds' dances are sometimes performed to perk things up.

Jazz at the Gulbenkian

Concerts and Dance. Lisbon's cultural scene offers occasional opera, symphony concerts, ballet and recitals, usually held in winter. The city's opera company is well regarded, and the Gulbenkian Foundation *(see page 54)* maintains its own symphony orchestra and ballet company.

Portugal has three other important symphony orchestras and a national dance company. Soloists and ensembles from many countries also perform here.

Venues include: Coliseu dos Recreios (Rua das Portas de Santo Antão 96; tel: 213 240 580), the second-largest music and events hall in Lisbon; Pavilhão Atlântico (Parque das Nações; tel: 218 919 333; <www.parquedasnacoes.pt>), the place for big-time rock bands and Brazilian acts; Fundação Calouste Gulbenkian (Av. de Berna 45; tel: 217 823 000), which hosts varied recitals, classical music and dance programmes, including open-air concerts in summer; Teatro Nacional de São Carlos (Rua Serpa Pinto 9; tel: 213 253 000),

Lisbon's opera house; and Centro Cultural de Belém (Praça do Império; tel: 213 612 400), which has a wide programme of cultural performances.

Theatre and Cinema. Most of Lisbon's stage plays are comedies and revues – in Portuguese, of course. The best-known theatre is **Teatro Nacional de Dona Maria II** (Praça de Dom Pedro IV/ Rossio; tel: 213 250 800).

Cinemas tend to show foreign films in the original language with Portuguese subtitles. **São Jorge** (Av. Liberdade 175; tel: 213 103 400) is a pleasantly renovated cinema housing three screens, and often hosts festivals.

Gambling. The **Estoril Casino** (tel: 214 667 700; *see page 71*) is the big draw for gamblers. To enter the gaming rooms you have to pay a fee and show your passport. The casino is open daily 3pm–3am (closed Good Friday and Christmas Eve). A sign suggests that gentlemen wear jackets after 8pm, but no rules are enforced.

SPORTS

From swimming and hiking to deep-sea fishing, sports enthusiasts have plenty of options in the Lisbon area. The temperate climate also means year-round golf and tennis. If you're interested in diving or water skiing, or any other sport for which you need to hire equipment, ask at the tourist information offices in each town about the best places to do so.

Active Sports

Diving. Just off Sesimbra, south of Lisbon, the clear, calm waters are very good for snorkelling and scuba diving.

Fishing. All along the coast you will see anglers in boots casting off from the beaches, and others perched on rocks or man-made promontories. The best deep-sea fishing is for swordfish around Sesimbra.

Marina at Belém, with the Centro Cultural de Belém

Golf. The Lisbon and Tagus Valley area has 18 courses, including top-rated Estoril Golf Club (18 holes), one of the oldest in the country, at Estoril, tel: 214 660 367; Golf Estoril Sol (9 holes) near Sintra, tel: 219 232 461; Lisbon Sports Club (18 holes) at Belas near Queluz, tel: 214 310 077; and Quinta da Marinha (18 holes) near Cascais, designed by Robert Trent Jones, tel: 214 860 141.

For information on golf courses in the Lisbon area, visit <www.estorilsintragolfe.net>.

Riding. You can hire a horse, with or without an instructor, at the Belas Clube de Campo or at the Quinta da Marinha (see Golf, above), which also has an equestrian centre, tel: 214 869 600. In Sintra, several of the upmarket hotels, including Quinta da Capela and Tivoli Palácio de Seteais *(see pages 135–6)*, offer horse riding through local operators.

Sailing and Boating. Most beaches protected from the open ocean have rowing boats, canoes or pedalos for rent by the hour. Experienced sailors in search of a more seaworthy craft should ask at the local yacht marina. Rowing boats are also available at Parque das Nações near the Oceanário.

Swimming. Because of pollution along the Estoril Coast, you should not swim any closer to Lisbon than at Estoril itself, which has been granted an EU blue flag. At Guincho and beyond, the sea is perfectly clean and quite safe for swimming, but beware of the strong undertow. South of Lisbon from Caparica onwards is delightful, but can also be windy, with very rough seas.

Ask at the government tourist office for the leaflet on Portuguese beaches, with maps and details of facilities.

Tennis. Major hotels tend to have their own tennis courts, but there are tennis clubs and public courts as well. The Tivoli Lisboa in Lisbon is one of the rare city hotels with tennis courts on the premises. Many golf clubs also have their own courts, including Quinta da Marinha (tel: 214 860 050).

Spectator Sports

Bullfights. Portuguese bullfighting follows a style called *Arte Marialva*. Unlike Spanish bullfights, the bull – its horns sheathed – is not killed. There's artistry in the partnership between the splendidly dressed *cavaleiro* and his horse but, as barbed darts are planted into the bull's upper back, bullfighting remains a bloody spectacle. The horseman is aided by a back-up team, *peões de brega*, with distracting capes. They are succeeded in the arena by an eight-man team of volunteer *forcados*, wearing tight breeches, white stockings and short coat, who face the bull barehanded. All performers are judged on skill, style and courage. At the end the bull is led away among farm steers and is afterwards butchered.

Lisbon's **Campo Pequeno Praça de Touros** bullring (tel: 217 936 601; Metro: Campo Pequeno), at the top of Avenida da República, is a Victorian red-brick landmark with mock-Moorish arches and bulbous domes. The **Monumental** arena in Cascais is bigger, but a bullfighter hasn't made it until he conquers the fans at Campo Pequeno.

The season runs from Easter Sunday to October. As in Spain, seats in the shade *(sombra)* cost more than in the sun *(sol)*, though there are performances in the evening as well. For a modicum of comfort, rent a pillow from the usher.

Car Racing. Although Portugal no longer hosts a Formula One Grand Prix, other motor races and events take place at Estoril's Autodrome.

Football (Soccer). Football draws big crowds in Portugal. Lisbon's two major teams are Benfica, which plays at the Estádio da Luz, rebuilt to hold the finals of the 2004 European championship, and Sporting Clube de Portugal, which holds matches at Estádio do José Alvalade near Campo Grande, and was also revamped for the championship.

Bullfighting Portuguese style

CHILDREN'S ACTIVITIES

With its trams, elevators, funiculars, ferries and tourist trains, Lisbon offers some great ways to entertain children just by touring around the city. The Transtejo ferry is a two-hour river trip that you can break at Belém or the **Parque das Nações**, which has a splendid aquarium (Oceanário de Lisboa, *see page 59*), playgrounds, fountains, paddleboats and aerial cable cars. The **Planetário Calouste Gulbenkian** in Belém *(see page 49)*, where there is a tourist train, has special planetarium shows for children on Sunday mornings.

North of the aqueduct is **Jardim Zoológico de Lisboa** (Zoo, Estrada de Benfica 158–60; tel: 217 232 900; Metro: Jardim Zoológico). Recently renovated to include new areas and larger spaces for the animals, the zoo goes to some effort to entertain younger visitors. There are elephant rides, boats and a miniature train, and shows at various times of day when animals from parrots to dolphins are fed. There is also a **wildlife park** with deer, wolves and boar at Mafra (open Mon–Fri 9.30am–3.30pm). **Campo Grande**, situated between the zoo and the airport, is a popular park.

Clown on Rua Augusta

Palm, cedar and willow trees shade pretty walks, and there's a small lake with rowing boats.

For a safe beach with clean water you'll have to travel some way from the city *(see page 90)*. Head for Guincho and Caparica when the wind is light, or Sesimbra and Tróia otherwise. Caparica has a water park with long, twisting slides.

Calendar of Events

As you plan your excursions, it is worth checking details of festivals and fairs in and around Lisbon with tourist information offices.

February Lisbon: *fado* festival at various sites in the city.

February–March Carnival (Mardi Gras). Celebrations include processions and nightly firework displays.

March–April Holy Week. Palm Sunday, Good Friday and Easter Day services and processions.

April–May Estoril Open Tennis Championship.

May Pilgrimage to Fátima (12–13 May), in which many locals take part.

May–Sept Bullfighting season, with a regular programme of events at the Moorish-style Campo Pequeno in the north of the city.

June Lisbon: festival of music, dance and theatre (all month). Lisbon: *festas dos santos populares* (festivals of the popular saints) starting with St Anthony (13 June). On the eve of his feast day there's a costumed parade down the Avenida da Liberdade followed by celebrations in Alfama, where music plays and people dance in the brightly decorated streets and squares. Wine flows in abundance, and sardines are grilled by the thousand. The nights of St John (23 June) and St Peter (28 June) are almost as festive, and the season finishes with a burst of fireworks. Cascais: the *Festa do Mar* (Festival of the Sea) between 12–29 June to coincide with the *festas dos santos populares*.

July Sintra: music festival, including live performances in the town's historic palaces and gardens (second week).

July–August Estoril and Cascais: Estoril International Music Festival. Cascais: Cascais Jazz Festival (first two weekends). Setúbal: Festival of Santiago, fair and exhibition.

August Sintra: Ballet Festival at Hotel de Seteais.

October Estoril: Estoril Open Golf Tournament.

November *Dia de São Martinho* (St Martin's Day), when the year's new wine is tasted. Lisbon: ATP Tour Masters Tennis World Championship.

December Lisbon: *Bolsa de Natal* Christmas market (throughout city).

EATING OUT

Seafood is perhaps the best thing to try in Lisbon, as there is a surfeit of fresh fish and shellfish. Not that restaurants skimp on meat: you can find delicious pork or lamb dishes and steak. More adventurous palates can try cuisines imported from Portugal's former African and Asian colonies. You'll also enjoy fresh fruit and vegetables, not to mention Portuguese wines, which are eminently drinkable.

Portions in Portuguese restaurants tend to be on the generous side. You can ask for a half portion (which is usually charged at approximately two-thirds the full price).

Alfresco in the Baixa

Restaurants and Menus

Government inspectors rate all Portuguese restaurants in four categories or *classes*. In descending order the classes are: *luxo* (luxury), *primeira* (first), *segunda* (second) and *terceira* (third). The scale is as much as anything an indicator of how costly a meal is likely to be. A rating sign is often displayed outside restaurants, while menus shown in the window or beside the door let you know what to expect in variety and price. Prices normally include taxes and a service charge, but you are expected

to leave an extra 5 to 10 percent tip for good service.

Whether you indulge in
one of Lisbon's chic new
riverfront restaurants or
absorb some local colour in
a humble fishermen's hang-
out (where you'll often find
the best food), you are
likely to come across a variety of dishes and prepara-
tions entirely new to you.

Many restaurants and
cafés offer an *ementa turística* – literally a 'tourist

Free appetisers?

Most restaurants serve
a *couvert* – unrequested
appetisers such as cheese,
ham and meat and fish
pastes that appear to be
free. They are not. You will
be charged a few euros for
these, but some, such as
shellfish, can be much more
expensive. If you do not
touch them, you should not
be charged for them. You
may have to point this out;
few people opt to abstain.

menu'. However, the term does not connote a poor-grade
meal of easily identifiable international dishes, targeting
tourists who'll never again set foot in the restaurant. Rather,
it is an economically priced set meal – typically bread, butter, soup, main course and dessert.

The prices displayed outside some of Lisbon's cafés may
apply only if you stand at the bar. In Portugal, as in some
other European countries, if you sit down at a table, you will
have to pay the higher prices quoted on the regular menu.
Also, in restaurants where seafood portions are charged by
weight, waiters may bring out repeated portions without
your specifically ordering more. If you don't refuse them
early on, the bill might be quite a shock.

Mealtimes

Breakfast *(pequeno almoço)* is usually eaten any time up
until about 10am. **Lunch** *(almoço)* is served from shortly
after noon until 3pm, and **dinner** *(jantar)* runs from 7.30 to
9.30pm (or later in a *casa de fado*). Snacks between meals

Inside Café A Brasileira

are usually taken at a *pastelaria* (pastry and cake shop), *salão de chá* (tea shop), or what the Portuguese call, in English, a *snack bar* – an over-the-counter bar, selling sandwiches, savoury pastries and sweets.

Because lunch and dinner tend to be major events, you may prefer the kind of light breakfast the Portuguese eat: coffee, toast or rolls, butter and jam. Larger hotels usually provide all the extras – such as juice, cereal, eggs, bacon – in American-style buffets.

Local Specialities

Soups. Lunch and dinner often get off to a solid start, and soups are hale-and-hearty typical Portuguese fare. *Caldo verde* (green soup) is a thick broth of potato purée with finely shredded cabbage or kale. Sometimes sausage is added. *Sopa à Portuguesa* is similar to *caldo verde*, but with added broccoli, turnips, beans, carrots and anything else the cook happens to have to hand. *Sopa de cozido* is a rich meat broth with cabbage and perhaps macaroni added. (This course is often followed by *cozido*, a huge serving of all the things that were boiled to create the broth, including beef, chicken, pork, sausages, potatoes, cabbage and carrots.) *Canja de galinha* is simple chicken-and-rice soup.

Seafood. The best advertisement for seafood is usually the window of a restaurant: a generous refrigerated display case with crabs and prawns, oysters and mussels, sea bass and sole. Seafood restaurants generally sell shellfish by the weight, giving the price in euros per kilo. The Portuguese are very fond of boiled and grilled fish dishes, usually served with generous portions of cabbage and boiled potatoes and doused with a little oil and vinegar.

A number of seafood dishes are true local specialities. *Caldeirada* is a rich seafood stew. *Amêijoas na cataplana* is an invention from the Algarve, of steamed clams (or mussels) with sausages, tomato, white wine, ham, onion and herbs. *Açorda de marisco* is a spicy, garlic-scented thick bread soup full of seafood bits; raw eggs are later added to the mixture. *Lulas recheadas* are squid stuffed with rice, olives, tomato, onion and herbs, though large squid *(chocos)* are often simply grilled. *Lampreia à Minho* is lamprey, not always highly regarded, but quite a delicacy in Portugal, served with a bed of rice and red wine sauce (best from January to March). *Sardinhas* (sardines) are excellent in Lisbon and often served charcoal-grilled *(sardinhas assadas)*.

Bacalhau (cod) is the national dish of Portugal, even though it can be expensive nowadays, and comes dried and salted, and from distant seas. The Portuguese say that cod is served in 100, 365 or

Salt and pepper

Salt and pepper are seldom put on the table. However, you will be given them if you ask:
Sal e pimenta, faz favor.

Market price

If you see 'preço V' (or simply 'PV') beside the seafood or shellfish on a menu, it means that the price is variable depending on the day's market price. Ask the price before ordering.

1,000 different ways, depending on the teller's taste for hyperbole. One of the best ways to try it is in *Bacalhau à Gomes de Sá*, in which flaky chunks are baked with parsley, potatoes, onion and olives and garnished with crumbled hard-boiled egg.

Fresh fish, whole or filleted, is usually served grilled, as are *atum* (tuna) and *espadarte*, swordfish steaks. For those who know some Spanish or Portuguese, *peixe espada* might sound like swordfish; however, it is actually scabbard fish, a long, thin fish that comes from the area south of Lisbon.

Meat. *Bife na frigideira* is not what you might think. *Frigideira* means frying pan, and this dish is beefsteak cooked in a wine sauce. *Cabrito assado* is baked kid served with rice and potato, heavy going but delicious. *Carne de porco à Alentejana* is an inspired dish of clams and pork cooked with paprika and garlic. *Espetada mista* means Portuguese shish kebab: chunks of beef, lamb and pork on a spit. *Feijoada* is the national dish of Brazil, the former Portuguese colony. In Portugal, it's not nearly as elaborate or ritualised, but it's still a hearty and tasty stew of pigs' feet and sausage, white beans and cabbage.

Note that the majority of meat dishes are served with *both* rice and potatoes.

Game and Fowl. *Frango* (chicken) is popular and prepared many ways: stewed in wine sauce, fried, roasted and barbecued to a tasty crisp. Some restaurants specialise in game – *codorniz* (quail), *perdiz* (partridge), *lebre* (hare) and even *javali* (wild boar).

Dessert and Cheese. The Portuguese sweet tooth may be a little too much for your taste. Locals pour sugar on a sliced sweet orange, for instance. Portuguese cakes, custards and pastries made with egg yolks and sugar are delicious. *Pudim flan* is the Portuguese version of crème caramel. *Arroz doce* is rice pudding with a dash of cinnamon. *Maçã assada* is a tasty sugary baked apple. *Pudim Molotov* sounds like a bomb, and indeed it's so rich that it's sure to explode any strict diet. The fluffy egg-white mousse is immersed in a sticky caramel sauce.

For those whose waistlines are wary of such indulgence, there's always cheese. The richest and most expensive in Portugal is *Serra da Estrela*, a delicious cured ewe's-milk cheese that originates high up in the mountains. Also on many menus is *Flamengo*, a mild cheese very similar to Edam. Some restaurants serve *queijo fresco* as an appetiser. This is a small, white, soft mini-cheese made of ewe's and goat's milk, but it's fairly bland, so you may want to season it with pepper and salt.

Custard tarts from Belém

International and Exotic Cuisine

Portugal's imperial legacy means that you can experiment with different cuisines while you're in Lisbon. The former colony of Goa accounts for the local popularity of *caril* (curry) and other Indian-style dishes. A typical Goan delicacy, a lot less pungent than Indian food, is *xacuti* (pronounced and sometimes spelled *chacuti*). The dish is simply chunks of fried chicken in a sauce of pepper, coriander, saffron, cinnamon, cumin, anise, cloves and coconut milk served with steamed rice. *Piri-piri* is a hot-pepper condiment and preparation from Angola that will set most mouths ablaze. Order a *piri-piri* dish with extreme caution.

Four centuries of ties with the territory of Macau assures all lovers of Chinese food a night out with dishes such as *gambas doces* (sweet-and-sour prawns).

Drinks: Table Wines

Portuguese wines are on the whole quite good, and several regions produce truly excellent wines. Ask the waiter for *tinto* (red) or *branco* (white).

Vinho verde (green wine), produced in the northwest, is like a young white wine, but fizzy, light and delightful. A lesser-known type is a red wine from the same region, bearing the seemingly oxymoronic name *vinho verde tinto* (red green wine). Both of these wines should be served chilled, as should Portuguese rosé, which is also slightly bubbly, and may be either sweet or very dry. *Vinhos maduros* are mature, or aged, wines.

Vintage port

A bottle of vintage port should be consumed within 48 hours of opening. At home or in Portugal, don't pay a high price for a glass of a rare vintage port unless the bartender or waiter opens the bottle in front of you. For most establishments, that's too expensive a proposition.

Vinho espumante is Portuguese sparkling wine, packaged in a Champagne-shaped bottle. Most are sweet, but you can also find some quite dry versions.

All of the best wine-producing regions have names whose use is controlled by law *(região demarcada)*. You may come across these classifications: Bucelas, a light and fresh white wine; Colares, a traditional red wine; and Setúbal, a mellow, sweet white, sometimes served as an aperitif. Dão and Douro in the north produce vigorous reds and flavourful whites. Wines from the Alentejo region are also highly regarded.

The two most celebrated Portuguese wines, port and Madeira, are mostly known as dessert wines, but they may also be sipped as aperitifs. The before-dinner varieties are dry or extra-dry white port and the dry Madeiras, *Sercial* and *Verdelho*. These should be served slightly chilled. After dinner, sip one of the famous tawny ports (aged tawnys are especially good), or a Madeira dessert wine, *Boal* or *Malvasia* (malmsey).

Cervejeria da Trindade

Other Drinks

Portuguese beers are good and refreshing. Light or dark, they are served chilled, bottled or from the tap. One of the best and most common brands is Sagres. *Aguardente* (literally 'fire water') is the local brandy. *Aguardente velha* (old) is a fine digestif.

Coffee and Tea

Coffee is the main choice of beverage during the day and at the end of lunch or dinner. Most people order a *bica*, a small cup of black espresso coffee – also called simply *um café* or *um café espresso*.

Tea (*chá*, pronounced 'shah'), by the bag, is also drunk – after all, it was the Portuguese explorers who first introduced it to the rest of the Western world. Although the concept of afternoon tea is generally regarded as British, its origins are in fact Portuguese, dating from 1662, when Catherine of Bragança, sister of Dom Afonso VI, married the English King Charles II. Her fashionable court popularised tea drinking.

Port and Madeira

Thanks to the unique growing conditions of the Douro Valley in the north of Portugal, fortified port wine has tantalised palates around the world since the British began exporting it in the 17th century. It differs from other wines due to the microclimate and soil of the region, and to the fact that the fermentation process is stopped with brandy. Around 10 percent of the grapes picked each year are still crushed in treading rooms by barefoot men. After two or three days' fermentation the brandy is added. The following spring, the fortified wine is sent to mature at the lodges on the banks of the River Douro at Vila Nova de Gaia (opposite Porto), from where it is shipped.

First produced on the island of Madeira in the 15th century, Madeira wine became an important export trade due to a combination of its notable quality and Madeira's position on the shipping lanes to the Indies. With the rise of the British colonies in North America and the West Indies, it fast became a favourite on both sides of the Atlantic. Madeira wine only became a fortified wine when, like port, it was decided to add grape brandy to stabilise it on long sea voyages.

To Help You Order…

Could we have a table?	**Queremos uma mesa.**
Do you have a set-price menu?	**Tem uma ementa turística?**
I'd like a/an/some…	**Queria…**

beer	**uma cerveja**	napkin	**guardanapo**
the bill	**a conta**	pepper	**pimenta**
bread	**pão**	potatoes	**batatas**
butter	**manteiga**	salad	**salada**
dessert	**sobremesa**	salt	**sal**
fish	**peixe**	sandwich	**sanduíche**
fruit	**fruta**	soup	**sopa**
ice-cream	**gelado**	sugar	**açúcar**
meat	**carne**	tea	**chá**
the menu	**a carta**	vegetables	**legumes**
milk	**leite**	wine	**vinho**
mineral water	**água mineral**	wine list	**carta de vinhos**

… and Read the Menu

alho	garlic	**lombo**	fillet
amêijoas	baby clams	**lulas**	squid
arroz	rice	**mariscos**	shellfish
assado	roast, baked	**mexilhões**	mussels
bacalhau	cod	**ostras**	oysters
besugo	sea bream	**ovo**	egg
dobrada	tripe	**pescada**	hake
dourada	sea-bass	**pescadinha**	whiting
feijões	beans	**polvos**	baby octopus
frito	fried	**queijo**	cheese
gambas	prawns	**salmonete**	red mullet
lagosta	spiny lobster	**truta**	trout
lenguado	sole	**vitela**	veal

HANDY TRAVEL TIPS

An A–Z Summary of Practical Information

A Accommodation . . 105
  Airport 105
B Budgeting for
  Your Trip 106
C Camping 107
  Car Hire 108
  Climate 109
  Clothing 109
  Crime and Safety . 109
  Customs and Entry
  Requirements . . . 110
D Driving 111
E Electricity 114
  Embassies and
  Consulates 114
  Emergencies 114
G Gay and Lesbian
  Travellers 115
  Getting There 115
  Guides and Tours . 117

H Health and
  Medical Care . . . 117
  Holidays 118
L Language 119
M Maps 121
  Media 121
  Money 121
O Opening Hours . . . 122
P Police 123
  Post Offices 123
  Public Transport . . . 124
R Religion 126
T Telephones 126
  Time Zones 127
  Tipping 127
  Toilets 128
  Tourist
  Information 128
W Websites 129
Y Youth Hostels 129

A

ACCOMMODATION (see also CAMPING, YOUTH HOSTELS and the list of RECOMMENDED HOTELS on page 130)

Except for family-run *hotéis rurais,* hotels in Portugal are graded from 2-star to 5-star de luxe. The rates are lower in a less elaborate hostelry: an *estalagem* or inn; a *pensão* (rooms with meals available); or *residencial* (rooms, generally without meals). Confusingly, even some elite, intimate inns are often referred to as a *pensão.*

Pousadas are a chain of establishments usually in historic buildings and scenic sites, aimed at acquainting visitors with traditions in different parts of the country. Special attention is given to local food and wine as well as to the architecture and handicrafts of the region. Ask at tourist offices *(see page 128)* for a detailed list, or see the website <www.pousadas.pt>.

When you arrive at your accommodation, you'll usually be asked for your passport and to sign a form which sets out the conditions, prices and room number. Breakfast may be included in the total cost.

a double/single room	**um quarto duplo/simples**

AIRPORT (*aeroporto;* see also GETTING THERE)

The Aeroporto de Lisboa is only 6km (4 miles) from the city centre, a 15-minute drive (allow twice as long at rush hour). There is a helpful tourist information office at the airport.

Bus 91, the AeroBus airport shuttle, leaves about every 20 minutes, 7.45am–8.45pm. It passes through the city centre, stopping at Rossio on the way to Cais do Sodré train station. The ticket (€3, on board €1.20) can be used all day on trams and buses (though not the Metro). Taxis are plentiful, and charge about €10 to the centre of Lisbon.

The AeroBus shuttle also picks up passengers at selected hotels throughout Lisbon. Check with your hotel.

The main telephone number for the airport is 218 413 500. For information on flight times call 707 213 141.

Where do I get the bus to the airport/to the centre of Lisbon?	**Onde posso apanhar o autocarro para o aeroporto/para o centro da cidade?**

B

BUDGETING FOR YOUR TRIP

Accommodation. At top levels, hotels in Lisbon compare to those in other large European cities. Still, there are some good prices to be found. A 2-star hotel should be €60 or less for a double; a 3-star €60–100; and for a 4-star, expect to pay up to €175. In three categories – historic, design and monuments – *pousadas* are usually priced like 4-star hotels, though the most in-demand historic ones may go higher. Prices usually drop in winter (1 November–1 April). Most prices do not include breakfast but do include 5 percent IVA tax (VAT).

Airport transfer. The shuttle bus service costs €3; a taxi will cost around €10.

Car rental. Prices for a compact car with manual transmission, air conditioning, unlimited mileage and mandatory liability insurance usually start between €200 and €250 per week. This figure does not include collision-damage waiver insurance. Fuel is about €1.2 a litre.

Entertainment. Nightclub and disco covers are high (€10–20), as are drinks once inside (€7.50 and up). Concert tickets generally range from €10–45.

Flights. Around £150–300 from London.

Local transport. Public transport within the city – buses, trams and the Metro – is inexpensive, with single Metro fares at €0.75 a single ticket, and taxis are affordable and a good way to get around (especially up all those hills). Most taxi rides within Lisbon's major neighbourhoods will cost no more than €6. Trains to the Estoril Coast are inexpensive (Sintra, €3.60).

Meals. Even top-rated restaurants may be affordable compared to most European capitals. Portugal offers a midday meal bargain, the *menu* or *ementa turística*, often no more than €10–15 for a fixed-price, three-course meal. Portuguese wines are good and attractively priced (€10–20), even in fine restaurants. The house wine *(vinho da casa)* is normally good. A three-course dinner in a moderately priced restaurant (for one, with wine) should cost between €20 and €30. For an expensive meal in one of Lisbon's prestigious restaurants, expect to pay €50 and up per person.

Museums. Admission fees range about €2.50–5; some days are free. Other sites and attractions may cost between €5 and €10. A Lisboa Card *(see page 9)* gives discounts.

Sports. Golfing can be expensive, though the courses are excellent: green fees go up to €125. Horse riding is up to €50 a session.

C

CAMPING *(campar)*

There are several campsites in the Lisbon area. Facilities range from basic to elaborate (pools, tennis courts, bars and restaurants). **Camping Lisboa** (Parque Municipal de Campismo de Monsanto) has 400 individual camping bays and additional bungalows, swimming pool, tennis courts and mini-golf. It's located in Monsanto Park, at Estrada de Circunvalação 1500; tel: 217 628 200; fax 217 628 299.

Information can be obtained from tourist offices *(see page 128)* or the Federação Portuguesa de Campismo, Avenida Coronel Eduardo Galhardo 24D; tel: 218 126 890; <www.fcmportugal.com>.

May we camp here?	**Podemos acampar aqui?**
We have a caravan (trailer).	**Nós temos uma roulotte.**

CAR HIRE (automóveis de aluguer, see also DRIVING)

If you wish to travel a good deal around the Lisbon area and see it at your leisure, hiring a car is advisable. Major international firms Avis, Hertz, Budget, National and Europcar are located both at the airport and in Lisbon; sometimes they also have small satellite offices in other towns. Hotels may recommend local, inexpensive operators. Many companies offer discounts if you book over the internet in advance.

The minimum age for hiring a car is 21, and anyone hiring one must have held a valid licence for at least one year. Rental companies will accept your home country's national driver's licence, and you must show your passport. Third-party insurance should be included in the basic charge, but a collision-damage waiver and personal accident policy may be added.

A sub-compact, four-door car with manual transmission, air conditioning, unlimited mileage and mandatory liability insurance usually costs between €200 and €250 per week. Costs may rise in high season (Easter and summer months). Pick-up and drop-off at different points is acceptable without surcharge, though doing either at the airport will incur a supplement.

I'd like to hire a car today/tomorrow.	**Queria alugar um carro para hoje/amanhã.**
for one day/a week	**por um dia/uma semana**
Please include full insurance.	**Que inclua um seguro contra todos os riscos, por favor.**

To obtain the lowest rates available you'll need to arrange for a hire car in your home country. Ask for special seasonal rates and discounts, and make sure you find out what insurance is included. Many credit cards automatically include full collision coverage if you use the card to pay for the car, but be sure to verify this before

departure. Damage caused to the car by your own errors – or any
unattributable dents or scratches – will have to be paid for.

CLIMATE

Lisbon has an Atlantic climate influenced by the Mediterranean,
which produces hot summers and mild winters. Spring and autumn
are the best seasons to be in Lisbon, but in the summer, you can
bask in the sunshine at the beaches west and south of the capital.
The table below gives average air temperates per month.

	J	F	M	A	M	J	J	A	S	O	N	D
°C	12	12	14	15	18	21	23	24	22	18	15	13
°F	54	54	57	59	64	69	73	75	72	64	59	55

CLOTHING (roupa)

Unless you come to Lisbon in an unseasonably cold winter, you'll
never really have to dress warmly. Spring and autumn are relatively balmy, so you won't need anything heavier than a sweater in the
daytime and light jacket at night. Summer days can be quite hot,
but pack a wrap or sweater for cooler, windy evenings, and rain-
wear, just in case. A folding umbrella is useful in the winter months.

Lisboetas dress fashionably but not formally. Virtually no establishments require a tie. The Estoril Casino 'recommends' that men
wear jackets in the evenings.

Will I need a tie?	**É preciso gravata?**
Is it all right if I wear this?	**Vou bem assim?**

CRIME AND SAFETY (see also EMERGENCIES and POLICE)

Lisbon traditionally has been one of Europe's more laid-back and
safe cities, but you should still take the usual precautions. Carry

valuables in inside pockets and keep your handbag or camera bag firmly under your arm. Stay alert for pickpockets on buses, trams and in cafés on Rossio, the Alfama area, markets and other tourist spots.

In most parts of the Baixa and Bairro Alto, it is safe to walk at night. The occasionally seedy Rossio square and narrow, dark and easy-to-get-lost-in streets of the Alfama district are best avoided at night; if you are going to a *fado* house in the latter, it's wise to take a taxi and have one called when you leave.

The beaches of the Estoril Coast outside Lisbon are quite safe, but it is not a good idea to take any valuables, cameras or purses to the beach.

As a general rule, keep valuables in the hotel safe, and refrain from carrying large sums of money or wearing expensive jewellery. Report any theft to the hotel receptionist, the nearest police station or the local tourist office. Leave nothing of value in parked cars, the easiest target for thieves; always lock cars and never leave cases, bags, cameras, etc. in view.

| I want to report a theft. | **Quero participar um roubo.** |

CUSTOMS AND ENTRY REQUIREMENTS *(alfândega/vistos)*

American, Australian, British, Canadian and many other nationalities need only a valid passport for a visit to Portugal. All European Union nationals merely need a national identity card. The length of stay authorised for most tourists is 90 days (60 for US and Canadian citizens).

Currency restrictions. Visitors from abroad can enter or exit Portugal with any amount of local or foreign currency, but sums exceeding the equivalent of €12,500 in foreign currency must be declared on arrival.

Customs. Free exchange of non-duty-free goods for personal use is permitted between Portugal and other countries in the EU. However, duty-free items are still subject to restrictions: be sure to check before you go.

I've nothing to declare.	**Não tenho nada a declarar.**
It's for my personal use.	**É para uso pessoal.**

D

DRIVING (see also CAR HIRE)

It is possible, but not advisable, to drive in Lisbon. Traffic is heavy and parking is extremely difficult. For most visitors, public transport and private taxis are vastly superior methods of navigating the city.

To bring your own car into Portugal, you will need your national driving licence, registration papers and insurance – third-party cover is obligatory – and the Green Card that makes your insurance valid in other countries.

Road conditions. The main roads of Portugal are generally in good repair. In order of importance, they are graded as follows: *Auto-Estrada*: motorways (A1–A2, etc.); *Itinerário Principal*:

Are we on the right road for...?	**É esta a estrada para...?**
Fill the tank, please	**Encha o depósito, se faz favor.**
Check the oil/tyres/battery, please.	**Verifique o óleo/os pneus/ a bateria, se faz favor.**
I've broken down.	**O meu carro está avariado.**
There's been an accident.	**Houve um acidente.**

highways (IP); *Itinerário Complementar*: Principal Route (IC); and *Estrada Nacional*: national roads (EN).

Rules and regulations. The rules of the road are the same as in most western European countries. Drive on the right. At round-abouts the vehicle already on the roundabout has priority unless road markings or lights indicate otherwise. Seat belts are compulsory and a heavy fine can be imposed if you are not wearing one. In towns, pedestrians nominally have priority at pedestrian crossings, and vehicles are generally courteous, but if you're walking, don't bank on it!

Speed limits are 120km/h (75mph) on motorways, 90km/h (56mph) on other roads and 50km/h (37mph) in urban areas. Minimum speeds are posted (in blue) for some motorway lanes and the suspension bridge across the Tagus. Most motorways have tolls.

Fuel costs. Fuel prices are controlled by the government, and should be the same, or very close to it, everywhere you go. Many fuel stations are 24-hour, and all accept credit cards. Unleaded petrol *(sem chumbo)* costs around €1.2 a litre; diesel fuel *(gasoleo)* costs around €1 a litre.

Parking. Unless there's an indication to the contrary, you can park for as long as you wish. Certain areas are metered. In 'Blue Zones', you must buy a ticket from a machine for a designated time period; the ticket should then be displayed on the dashboard of the parked car. Car parks and garages are also available.

If you need help. If you belong to a motoring organisation that is affiliated to the Automóvel Clube de Portugal (Rua Rosa Araújo 24, tel: 213 563 931, 808 502 502), you can use their emergency and repair services free of charge. You can also access information about the Club by visiting <www.acp.pt>.

Road signs. Standard international pictograms are used in Portugal, but you might also encounter the following signs:

alto	Halt
cruzamento	crossroads
curva perigosa	dangerous bend (curve)
descida ingreme	steep hill
desvio	diversion (detour)
encruzilhada	crossroads
estacionamento permitido	parking allowed
estacionamento proíbido	no parking
guiar com cuidado	drive with care
obras/fim de obras	roadworks (men at work)/ end of roadworks
paragem	bus stop
pare	stop
passagem proíbida	no entry
pedestres/peões	pedestrians
perigo	danger
posto de socorros	first-aid post
proíbida a entrada	no entry
saída de camiões	truck exit
seguir pela direita/esquerda	keep right/left
sem saída	no through road
sentido proíbido	no entry
sentido único	one-way street
silêncio	silence zone
stop	stop
trabalhos	roadworks (men at work)
trânsito proíbido	no through traffic
veículos pesados	heavy vehicles
velocidade máxima	maximum speed

E

ELECTRICITY *(corrente eléctrica)*

Standard throughout Portugal is 220v, 50-cycle AC. For US appliances, 220v transformers and plug adaptors are needed.

I need an adaptor/a battery, please.	**Preciso de um adaptador/ uma pilha, por favor.**

EMBASSIES AND CONSULATES *(consulado; embaixada)*

Most embassies and consulates are open Monday to Friday from 9 or 10am until 5pm, with a break in the middle of the day of 1–2 hours.

Australia: Avenida da Liberdade 198, 2°, tel: 213 101 500.
Canada: Avenida da Liberdade 196, 3°, tel: 213 164 600.
Ireland: Rua da Imprensa à Estrela 1, 4°, tel: 213 929 440.
South Africa: Avenida Luís Bivar 10, tel: 213 192 200.
UK: Rua de São Bernardo 33, tel: 213 924 000.
US: Avenida das Forças Armadas 16, tel: 217 273 300.

Where's the British/ American embassy? It's very urgent.	**Onde é a embaixada inglesa/ americana? É muito urgente.**

EMERGENCIES *(urgência; see also POLICE)*

The following numbers are useful 24 hours a day in an emergency:

General emergency	**112**
Police	**217 654 242**
Ambulance (Red Cross)	**219 421 111**
Emergency road service	**219 429 103**
Brisa (highways)	**808 508 508**

Although you can call the police from any one of the blue boxes in the street marked *polícia*, it's unlikely you'll get anyone on the other end who speaks anything but Portuguese.

G

GAY AND LESBIAN TRAVELLERS

In a country heavily influenced by the Roman Catholic Church, in Portugal attitudes towards gays and lesbians are not as tolerant as elsewhere in Europe.

Lisbon is the most important city in Portugal's gay scene, and offers a number of bars and clubs catering to a gay crowd, including Bar 106 (Rua de São Marcal 106) and Frágil (Rua da Atalaia 126). Also, on the Costa da Caparica, on the west coast of the peninsula across the Tagus, beach no. 9 on the narrow-gauge railway is gay.

As yet, there are no helplines. A good website with information in a number of languages is <www.portugalgay.pt>. It has information on travel, bars and beaches, and also has a message board.

GETTING THERE (see also AIRPORT)

By air. Lisbon's airport is linked by regularly scheduled daily non-stop flights from several European cities and from the East Coast of the United States. Flights from Canada, Australia and New Zealand go through London or another European capital.

TAP/Air Portugal (<www.tap.pt>) is Portugal's national airline, and it has wide international links: tel: 707 205 700 from anywhere in Portugal; in Lisbon, 218 415 000; in New York, 718 656 7455; in the UK, 0845 601 0932. There are regular TAP and British Airways (<www.ba.com>) scheduled flights from the UK to Lisbon. Budget airlines offering services from the UK to Lisbon include easyJet (from London Luton; <www.easyjet.com>), Monarch (London Gatwick; <www.flymonarch.com>) and Thomsonfly (Manchester; <www.

thomsonfly.com>). From the US to Lisbon, TAP flies direct from New York, Newark and Boston. Continental (<www.continental.com>) flies direct from Newark. There are flights to the Portuguese capital on TAP and other carriers from all major European cities.

By sea. Lisbon is a major port, and several cruise ships include a port of call in the capital, including *Celebrity, Renaissance, Princess, Norwegian* and *Royal Caribbean.*

Ferries from Great Britain go to Santander, Spain, from Plymouth and Portsmouth (Brittany Ferries; <www.brittany-ferries.com>), and to Bilbao, Spain, from Portsmouth (P&O Ferries; <www.poferries. com>). Crossings take 24–36 hours. The drive from northern Spain to Lisbon is then likely to take another 12–14 hours.

By rail. Portugal is linked to the European railway network and connections to Lisbon are possible from points throughout Spain, France and the rest of continental Europe. Travel to Portugal is included on the InterRail Global Pass (<www.interrailnet.com>) for Europeans, and the Eurail Global Pass (<www.eurail.com> for non-Europeans.

The Portuguese national railway network is called **Caminhos de Ferro Portugueses** (tel: 808 208 208 within Portugal, 213 185 990 outside Portugal; <www.cp.pt>). The Santa Apolónia station (Avenida Dom Henrique, tel: 218 816 242) serves all international trains.

Daily international trains run between Paris and Lisbon (Sud Express), crossing the frontier at Vilar Formoso; between Lisbon and Madrid, crossing the frontier at Marvão; and between Oporto and Vigo, crossing the frontier at Valença.

By car. Major motorways connect Portugal with Spain at numerous border points. The fastest route from Oporto is the A1 *auto-estrada*; from Madrid, take A2, crossing into the city at the Ponte 25 de Abril. The drive from Madrid to Lisbon is 8–10 hours; from Paris, 20–22 hours.

GUIDES AND TOURS *(guias, visitas guiadas)*

Information on tours currently on offer are available at tourist offices or from your hotel.

Carristour, operated by the city's bus company, has tram and bus tours starting in the Praça do Comércio. Trams travel the Circuito Descobrimentos to Belém and the Eléctrico das Colinas around the city hills; open-top buses go to the Parque das Nações and Belém.

A bus service called **Join us at** also leaves from Praça do Comércio and tours the city, stopping frequently.

Cityline open-top bus tours start from Praça Marquês de Pombal. Carristour also operates a four-hour sightseeing tour of Sintra.

All of the major excursion firms offer trips to Cascais, Estoril, Mafra, Queluz and Sintra, as well as a long day's outing covering major sites north of Lisbon: Fátima, Alcobaça and Batalha, Óbidos and Nazaré. If you are travelling independently, you can cover all these at greater leisure, even making an overnight stop or two on the way.

Transtejo offers 2-hour cruises on the River Tagus, going up to the Parque das Nações, then down to Belém, with brief stops at each. They leave from Terreiro do Paço, 1 April–31 October, daily at 3pm (€20; tel: 808 203 050, 213 224 000; <www.transtejo.pt>)

We'd like an English-speaking guide.	**Queremos um guia que fale inglês.**

H

HEALTH AND MEDICAL CARE

Standards of hygiene in Lisbon, and in Portugal as a whole, are generally very high; the most likely illness to befall travellers will be due to an excess of sun or alcohol. The water is safe to drink, but bottled water is available everywhere. Ask for *água com gas* (carbonated) or *sem gas* (still).

Farmácias (chemists/drugstores) are open during normal business hours, and one shop in each neighbourhood is on duty round the clock. Addresses are listed in newspapers and on pharmacy doors. To locate night pharmacies, call tel: 118.

For more serious illness or injuries, there is also a **British Hospital** (XXI, Rua Tomás da Fonseca Edifícios B e F, Torres de Lisboa, tel: 217 213 400; also at Campo de Ourique, tel: 213 943 100), which has English-speaking staff. Check your medical insurance to be sure it covers illness or accident while you are abroad. EU nationals with a European Health Insurance Card or EHIC, obtained before departure (from post offices or online at <www.ehic.org.uk> in the UK), can receive free emergency treatment at Social Security and Municipal hospitals in Portugal. Privately billed hospital visits are expensive.

I need a doctor/dentist	**Preciso de um médico/ dentista**
Get a doctor quickly.	**Chame um médico, depressa.**
Where's the nearest pharmacy?	**Aonde é a farmácia (de guardia) mais perto?**
an ambulance	**uma ambulância**
hospital	**hospital**
upset stomach	**mal de estômago**
sunstroke	**uma insolação**
fever	**febre**

HOLIDAYS *(feriado)*

1 January	*Ano Novo*	New Year's Day
25 April	*Dia da Liberdade*	1974 Revolution Day
1 May	*Dia do Trabalhador*	May Day
10 June	*Dia de Camões*	Camões's Day

15 August	*Assunção*	The Assumption
5 October	*Implantaçao da República*	Republic Day
1 November	*Todos-os-Santos*	All Saints' Day
1 December	*Dia da Independência*	Independence Day
8 December	*Imaculada Conceição*	Immaculate Conception
25 December	*Natal*	Christmas Day

Moveable dates

Carnaval (Shrove Tuesday/Carnival), *Sexta-feira Santa* (Good Friday) and *Corpo de Deus* (Corpus Christi).

Local holidays

Lisbon, Estoril and Cascais have a local holiday on 13 June in honour of St Anthony (Santo António). Sintra has a holiday on 29 June (São Pedro).

L

LANGUAGE

Portuguese, a derivative of Latin, is spoken in such far-flung spots as Brazil, Angola, Mozambique and Macau – all former colonies of Portugal. Any high-school Spanish may help with signs and menus, but will not unlock the mysteries of spoken Portuguese. The Portuguese spoken in Portugal is much more closed and gutteral-sounding, and is also spoken much faster than in Brazil.

Almost everyone in Portugal understands Spanish, many speak French and a surprising number of people in Lisbon can speak passable English. Schoolchildren are taught French and English.

The *Berlitz Portuguese Phrasebook & Dictionary* covers most situations you're likely to encounter during a visit to Portugal. Also useful is the *Berlitz Portuguese–English/English–Portuguese Pocket Dictionary,* containing a menu-reader supplement.

Some helpful phrases to get you going are:

Do you speak English?	**Fala inglês?**
excuse me/you're welcome	**perdão/de nada**
please	**faz favor**
thank you	**obrigado/a**
where/when/how	**onde/quando/como**
day/week/month/year	**dia/semana/mês/ano**
left/right	**esquerda/direita**
near/far	**perto/longe**
cheap/expensive	**barato/caro**
open/closed	**aberto/fechado**
hot/cold	**quente/frio**
old/new	**velho/novo**
Please write it down.	**Escreva-lo, por favor.**
What does this mean?	**Que quer dizer isto?**
Help me, please.	**Ajude-me, por favor.**
Just a minute.	**Um momento.**
What time is it?	**Que horas são?**

Days:

Sunday	**domingo**
Monday	**segunda-feira**
Tuesday	**terça-feira**
Wednesday	**quarta-feira**
Thursday	**quinta-feira**
Friday	**sexta-feira**
Saturday	**sábado**
What day is it today?	**Que dia é hoje?**
yesterday	**ontem**
today	**hoje**
tomorrow	**amanhã**

MAPS *(mapas)*

Tourist information offices have free maps of Lisbon and the surrounding area, as well as a Carris map of the tram, bus and elevator network. Towns on the tourist circuit, such as Óbidos, Sintra, Cascais and Estoril, also make free maps available through their tourist information offices.

MEDIA *(jornal, revista, rádio, televisão)*

Europe's principal newspapers, including most British dailies, and the *International Herald Tribune*, are available on the day of publication at many newsagents and hotels. Popular foreign magazines are also sold at the same shops or stands. The most important Portuguese-language daily is *Diário de Notícias*, which contains cultural listings.

Free listings publications, such as *Follow Me Lisboa, Agenda Cultural Lisboa* and *Tips,* are widely available. *Portugal News*, an English-language weekly published in the Algarve, covers stories from around the country (<www.portugalnews.com>).

Four television channels are widely available in Portugal: two are government-run and two are independent. Foreign films, whether made-for-TV or original cinematic productions, are usually shown in the original language with subtitles. Most hotels have access to satellite TV. The government operates four radio channels.

MONEY *(dinheiro)*

Currency *(moeda).* The euro (€) is the official currency used in Portugal. Notes are denominated in 5, 10, 20, 50, 100, 200 and 500 euros; coins in 1 and 2 euros and 1, 2, 5, 10, 20 and 50 cents (centimos).

Currency exchange *(banco, câmbio).* Normal banking hours are Mon–Fri 8.30am–3pm. There is a 24-hour exchange office at the airport; the exchange office at Santa Apolónia railway station is open 8.30am–8.30pm and the one in Praça dos Restauradores stays open 9am–8pm for the benefit of tourists.

Credit cards (*cartão de crédito*). International credit cards are widely accepted. However, in some shops and restaurants, especially in small towns outside Lisbon, you may not be able to use a credit card. Police fines cannot be paid by credit card.

ATMs (*caixa automática*). Automatic teller machines (ATMs) are the easiest method of obtaining euros, and provide the best exchange rates. They are widely available in Lisbon and its environs, usually located outside banks and identified by the MB (MultiBanco) sign.

Traveller's cheques. Less necessary now with the proliferation of ATMs, international traveller's cheques can be cashed at any bank for a substantial flat fee; be sure to bring your passport.

Tax refunds. For non-EU residents, the IVA tax (VAT) imposed on most goods can be refunded on purchases of at least €60 in a single store. Look for the blue-and-white tax-free sign in stores. To obtain the rebate, fill in a form provided by the shop where you purchase the goods. One copy is kept by the shop; the others must be presented at customs upon departure. The refund can be credited to your credit card at the airport or posted to your home address after your return.

Can I pay with this credit card?	**Posso pagar com cartão de crédito?**
I want to change some pounds/dollars.	**Queria trocar libras/dólares.**
Can you cash a traveller's cheque?	**Pode pagar um cheque de viagem?**

OPENING HOURS (*horas de abertura*)

Banks open 8.30am–3pm. The majority of shops and offices open 9/10am–1pm and 3–7pm weekdays, and Saturday 9am–1pm.

Most museums are closed on Monday and public holidays (the tourist office has a full list of those open on Monday); palaces are closed on either Monday or Tuesday. On every other day (including Sunday) they are open 10/11am–5pm, but many close noon–2pm or 1–2.30pm. A number of shopping centres around Lisbon and the suburbs have extended opening hours, closing at 10pm or midnight, including Sunday.

P

POLICE (*policia*; see also CRIME AND SAFETY and EMERGENCIES)

The Portuguese national police, identified by their blue uniforms, are generally helpful and friendly, and often speak a little English. Policemen assigned to traffic duty wear red armbands with a silver letter 'T' (for Trânsito, or traffic) on a red background, a white helmet and white gloves.

On highways, traffic is controlled by the Guarda Nacional Republicana (GNR) in white-and-red or white-and-blue cars, or on motorcycles. Occasionally they make spot-checks on documents or tyres, and can issue on-the-spot fines, payable in cash only.

Lisbon's police headquarters are in Largo Penha de França 1, 2nd floor, tel: 218 111 000. The emergency number is **112**.

Where's the nearest police station?	**Onde fica o posto de polícia mais próximo?**

POST OFFICES (*correios*)

The mail service is efficient, with British-style red pillar boxes. Local post offices are open Mon–Fri 9am–6pm. Major branch offices also operate on Saturday until noon. A 24-hour office can be found at the airport. Lisbon's main post office in Praça dos Restauradores (opposite the tourist office) opens Mon–Fri 9am–8pm, Sat, Sun and holidays 9am–1pm and 2–5pm. You can purchase stamps from some tobacconists and kiosks, and at post offices.

A stamp for this letter/ postcard, please.	**Um selo para esta carta/ este postal, por favor.**
airmail	**via aérea**

PUBLIC TRANSPORT *(transporte)*

Local buses. Bus stops have signs indicating the numbers of the buses that stop there; many give details of their routes. You can get a free map of the entire transit system at tourist information offices, or at information posts of Carris, the transport authority. Carris offices are at the base of the Santa Justa lift and Praça da Figueira. They also sell economical 1-day (€3.35) and 5-day (€13.20) passes *(bilhete/passe turístico)*, good on all buses and trams (but not the Metro), tel: 213-613 000. Most buses are entered from the front. Pay the driver or show him your prepaid ticket before putting it in the clipping machine.

Trams. Tram stops are indicated by large signs marked *paragem* (stop). The Carris bus map shows tram routes as well. The most popular tourist tram is the No. 28, which goes from Bairro Alto to Alfama and the castle. Most trams are entered at the front, where you buy a ticket from the driver. On funiculars you pay at the door.

Metro. Lisbon's underground railway system, the Metropolitano, is clean, modern and efficient, but it serves a limited area. It has four colour-coded lines, and a fifth is being built. The entry points are marked by an 'M' sign. Charts of the system are displayed in every station and carriage. Directions in several languages are posted in the stations. Economical 10-trip tickets, 1- and 7-day tickets *(bilhete um dia, bilhete sete dias)* are available. Insert tickets in the small (and sometimes easy-to-overlook) electronic gates at the entrance.

Trains *(comboio)*. Lisbon has four railway stations. The main ones for national and international travel are Santa Apolónia (reached by bus 9 or 9A from Avenida da Liberdade) and Estação do Oriente (Oriente Metro). Commuter trains for the western suburbs and Estoril and Cascais depart from Cais do Sodré, on the waterfront, while trains for Sintra and the west depart from Rossio station.

Taxis *(táxi)*. Lisbon's metered taxis, often Mercedes, are beige, and indicated by a sign reading TAXI. In rural areas, cars marked 'A' (meaning *aluguer,* 'for hire') operate as taxis without meters. Every neighbourhood has a taxi stand, as do most railway, Metro and ferry stations. The fare is shown on the meter – check that it's running. Drivers add 20 percent after 10pm and extra if you have over 30kg (66lb) of baggage. To request a taxi, tel: 218 119 000, 217 932 756 or 218 111 100.

How much is a ticket to…?	**Quanto é o bilhete para …?**
Will you tell me when to get off?	**Pode dizer-me quando devo descer?**
Where's the nearest bus/ tram stop?	**Onde fica a mais próxima paragem dos autocarros/ eléctricos?**
Where can I get a taxi?	**Onde posso encontrar um táxi?**
What's the fare to…?	**Quanto custa o percurso até …?**
bus	**autocarro**
car	**carro**
train	**comboio**
tram (trolley car)	**eléctrico**
subway/underground train	**Metro**

Ferries. The two main ferry stations for the River Tagus's southern shore are Estação Fluvial Terreiro do Paço for Barreiro, and Cais do Sodré for Cacilhas, Montijo and Seixal.

Inter-city buses. Lisbon's bus terminals serve different parts of the country. Ask for information about bus routes at the tourist office in Praça dos Restauradores. Long-distance buses are efficient and prices are quite reasonable.

R

RELIGION

The Portuguese are predominantly Roman Catholic, a fact reflected in surviving religious rituals and saints' days that are public holidays. The shrine at Fátima is one of the most important pilgrimages in Catholicism. The tourist information office has a list of services for English-speaking Catholics as well as other services.

T

TELEPHONES *(telefones)*

Portugal's country code is **351**. The local area code – **21** in the case of Lisbon and the Estoril Coast, including Sintra – must be dialled before all phone numbers, including local calls (nine digits in total).

Portugal public telephones (PT Comunicações) that accept both coins and prepaid telephone cards are found throughout the city. *Credifone* telephone cards can be purchased at post offices. Most phone boxes accept credit cards, an inexpensive and easy way of making any call. Local, national and international calls made from hotels almost always carry an exorbitant surcharge. Use an international calling card if you must call from your hotel room.

To call, pick up the receiver, insert card or coin, wait for the dial tone and dial the number. Dialling internationally is straightforward:

dial 00 for an international line (both Europe and overseas) plus the country code (UK 44, US 1) plus the phone number (including the area code, without the initial '0' where there is one). You can send a fax from most hotels, though the charge may well seem high.

For calls within Portugal, dial the entire number, including the area code.

collect call	**paga pelo destinatário**
Can you get me this number in...?	**Pode ligar-me para este número em...?**

TIME ZONES (hora local)

Portugal, being at the western edge of Europe, maintains Greenwich Mean Time (GMT), along with the UK, and is therefore one hour behind the rest of the EU. From the last Sunday in March until the last Sunday in October, the clocks are moved one hour ahead for summer time, GMT + 1.

In summer the chart looks like this:

New York	London	**Lisbon**	Paris	Sydney	Auckland
7am	noon	**noon**	1pm	9pm	11pm

TIPPING (serviço, gorjeta)

Hotel and restaurant bills are generally all-inclusive, but an additional tip of 5–10 percent is common, and may even be expected in some restaurants.

Hotel porters generally receive around €0.50–1 for each bag that they carry, while hairdressers and taxi drivers are normally tipped about 10 percent and tour guides 10–15 percent. Toilet attendants should be tipped about €0.25 and your hotel room cleaner should be given around an extra €0.50 per day.

TOILETS *(lavabo, quarto de banho, serviços)*

Public toilets can be found in many public places, including stations, museums and large stores. Almost every bar and restaurant has one available for public use. It's polite to buy a coffee or drink if you drop in to use the bathroom, but no one will shout at you if you don't.

Toilets are marked *Senhoras* (ladies) and *Homens* (men).

> Where are the toilets? **Onde é o lavabo/quarto de banho?**

TOURIST INFORMATION *(informação turística)*

Portuguese National Tourist Offices (ICEP, or Investimentos, Comércio e Turismo de Portugal; <www.turismodeportugal.pt>) are maintained in many countries, including the following:

Canada: Suite 1005, 60 Bloor Street West, Toronto, Ontario M4W 3B8, tel: 416 921 7376.
Ireland: 54 Dawson Street, Dublin, tel: 353 1670 9133.
South Africa: Mercantile Lisbon House, 142 West Street, Sandown 2196, Johannesburg, tel: 2711 302 0444.
UK: Portuguese Embassy, 11 Belgrave Square, London SW1X 8PP, tel: 020 7201 6666, 0845 355 1212.
US: 590 Fifth Ave, 4th floor, New York, NY 10036, tel: 212 764 6137.

The main tourist information office for the city is the **Lisboa Welcome Centre**, Rua do Arsenal 15, in Praça do Comércio, tel: 210-312 700. There is also a tourist office for the city as well as for the country in the **Palácio Foz**, on the west side of Praça dos Restauradores, tel: 213 221 200; also at the **Airport Arrivals Terminal** (tel: 218 439 799 or 808 209 209) and at **Santa Apolónia** station.

A useful tourist information **helpline** is available on tel: 800 781 212.

Where is the tourist office?	**Onde é o turismo?**

W

WEBSITES AND INTERNET CAFÉS *(cafés cibernéticos)*

The most useful websites are:

<www.visitlisboa.com> The Welcome Centre city tourist office
<www.visitportugal.com> The official Portuguese tourism site
<www.portugal.com> Travel and tourism site
<www.portugalvirtual.pt> General information and accommodation
<www.tap.pt> TAP/Air Portugal, the national airline
<www.cp.pt> Caminhos de Ferro Portugueses, the railway network
<www.pousadas.pt> For the government-owned *pousadas*

The Welcome Centre in Praça do Comércio has internet facilities and can give information on other *(ciber)* cafés all over the city. Central places include the PT Comunicações office (Praça dos Restauradores 68, open 8.30am–7.30pm) and Cibergate (Rua Cidade de Liverpool 16B, tel: 218 130 007).

Y

YOUTH HOSTELS

It is best to join Hostelling International before you depart (<www.hihostels.com>), but you can join up on arrival. The headquarters of the Portuguese Youth Hostel Association (Associação Portuguesa de Pousadas de Juventude) are at Rua Lúcio de Azevedo 27, Lisbon; tel: 217 232 100; reservations tel: 707 203 030; <www.pousadasjuventude.pt>. They run hostels in central Lisbon at Rua Andrade Corvo 46 (Metro: Picoas) , tel: 213 532 696, and in the Parque das Nações at Rua de Moscavide Lt 47–101 (Metro: Oriente), tel: 218 920 890.

Recommended Hotels

Hotel prices are relatively inexpensive for a European capital, except at the top level where they are on a par. Many hotels offer special packages, such as summer or weekend reductions. Central Lisbon covers the area from the waterfront, Bairro Alto, Lapa and Avenida da Liberdade. North Lisbon refers to the area around and beyond Praça Marquês de Pombal. *Pousadas*, found beyond Lisbon, are well-managed chain hotels; the ones listed occupy historic buildings, and their restaurants are usually among the town's best.

The price indication is for a double room, with breakfast, including service and taxes in high season (April–October). In low season prices can be considerably less. All the hotels take major credit cards unless otherwise stated.

€€€€€	over 200 euros
€€€€	150–200 euros
€€€	100–150 euros
€€	60–100 euros
€	below 60 euros

LISBON

Albergaria Senhora do Monte €€ *Calçada do Monte 39, tel: 218 866 002, fax: 218 877 783.* Perched on a hillside in Graça, a district northeast of Baixa, this simple-looking place offers good-value accommodation with excellent views of the castle and the river. Has a garden courtyard, where guests can have breakfast. 28 rooms.

As Janelas Verdes €€€–€€€€ *Rua das Janelas Verdes 47, tel: 213 968 143, fax: 213 968 144, <www.heritage.pt>.* A lovely, elegant hotel in the sophisticated Lapa district, near the River Tagus and the Museu de Arte Antiga. This small hotel occupies the 18th-century townhouse of one of Portugal's most famous writers, Eça de Queirós, and the home next door. It has a quiet, garden-like courtyard and top-floor library, and some rooms have superb views of the river. Wheelchair access. 29 rooms.

Bairro Alto Hotel €€€€€ *Praça Luís de Camões 2, tel: 213 408 288, fax: 213 408 299, <www.bairroaltohotel.com>*. Ultra-chic new hotel in the old heart of Lisbon. Rooms are soundproofed against city noise, and have plasma TVs and upmarket styling. 55 rooms.

Dom Pedro Lisboa €€€€ *Av. Eng. Duarte Pacheco 24, tel: 213 896 600, fax: 213 896 601, <www.dompedro.com>*. Lisbon's new five-star hotel, with the city's swankiest entrance, is this mirrored high-rise, just north of Parque Eduardo VII and across from the Amoreiras shopping mall. Rooms, equipped with every luxury, have spectacular views of the city. Dom Pedro has supplanted more traditional luxury hotels in Lisbon in just three years. Popular with American tourists and European business travellers. Top-flight Italian restaurant. Wheelchair access. 263 rooms.

Hotel Avenida Palace €€€€ *Rua 1 de Dezembro 123, tel: 213 218 100, fax: 213 422 884, <www.hotel-avenida-palace.pt>*. Situated right on Rossio, the major plaza in the Baixa district, the remodelled Avenida Palace is one of Lisbon's finest luxury hotels. Built in 1892 it has a magnificent Old World feel, with sumptuous public rooms and elegant, classically decorated accommodation. Sybarites can opt for the Louis XVI-style room. Wheelchair access. 82 rooms.

Hotel Borges €€ *Rua Garrett 108, tel: 213 461 951, fax: 213 426 617, <www.maisturismo.pt/1/2750.html>*. Typical old Lisbon hotel, a bit shabby but with a lot of character, in an excellent location right in the heart of the Chiado district. Spacious rooms include satellite TV. 96 rooms.

Hotel Britania €€€ *Rua Rodrigues Sampaio 17, tel: 213 155 016, fax: 213 155 021, <www.heritage.pt>*. Owned by the same family that runs two other top, intimate hotels in Lisbon, the Britania, in a historic 1940s townhouse, may be the most comfortable of them all. The rooms are spacious and elegantly appointed, with marble bathrooms. The hotel, near Avenida da Liberdade, has been lovingly restored and has gorgeous Art Deco touches, such as the bar. Wheelchair access. 30 rooms.

Hotel Métropole €€ *Praça do Dom Pedro V 30, tel: 213 219 030, fax: 213 469 166, <www.almeidahotels.com>*. One of Lisbon's best deals, this classic 1920s Art Deco hotel is situated in the heart of the Baixa, overlooking Rossio. Rooms are generously sized and outfitted with period antiques. Wheelchair access. 36 rooms.

Hotel Tivoli Lisboa €€€€ *Avenida da Liberdade 185, tel: 213 198 900, fax: 213 198 950, <www.tivolihotels.com>*. One of Lisbon's largest and longest-running luxury hotels, right on the main thoroughfare, Avenida da Liberdade. The Tivoli excels in services and facilities, which include a noted rooftop restaurant, a heated outdoor swimming pool and tennis courts – a real rarity in the city. Outdoor dining in summer. Wheelchair access. 327 rooms.

Hotel Veneza €€€ *Avenida da Liberdade 189, tel: 213 522 618, fax: 213 526 678, <www.3khotels.com>*. A small, historic hotel right on the main boulevard. This former 19th-century Venetian-style palace has a spectacular spiral staircase and period touches, such as stained-glass windows, throughout. Wheelchair access. 37 rooms.

Lapa Palace €€€€€ *Rua Pau da Bandeira 4, tel: 213 949 494, fax: 213 950 665, <www.lapa-palace.com>*. This lovingly detailed conversion of an old palatial mansion overlooks the River Tagus in Lapa. Opened in 1992, it remains the trendsetter in Lisbon luxury. Grounds are covered in landscaped gardens, and there is an outdoor pool. Rooms are plush, with *azulejo*-decorated bathrooms; the entrance, swathed in marble and ceiling frescos, is enough to make you swoon. Wheelchair access. 102 rooms.

Lisboa Plaza €€€ *Travessa do Salitre 7 (off Av. Liberdade), tel: 213 218 218, fax: 213 471 630, <www.heritage.pt>*. This stylish, renovated family-run hotel, on a quiet street off Avenida da Liberdade, opened in the 1950s. Rooms are very comfortable, with every detail carefully overseen by a noted Portuguese designer. A restaurant serves Portuguese specialities and a generous buffet breakfast. Wheelchair access. 116 rooms.

Lisboa Regency Chiado €€€ *Rua Nova do Almada 114, tel: 213 256 100, fax: 213 256 161, <www.regency-hotels-resorts.com>.* Opened in 2000, this chic hotel occupies part of the renovated building housing the Armazéns do Chiado shopping mall, in the heart of the Chiado district. In keeping with the upscale surroundings, the lobby and rooms are very design-orientated, with traditional Portuguese styling. There are superb views from the roof terrace. 40 rooms.

Pensão Londres € *Rua Dom Pedro V 53, tel: 213 462 203, fax: 213 465 682, <www.pensaolondres.com.pt>.* An unpretentious *pensão* at the edge of the Bairro Alto, occupying four floors of an imposing town house just minutes away from the district's restaurants, *fado* houses, bars and clubs. There are good views of the city from rooms on the 3rd and 4th floors; otherwise take in the vista from the nearby Miradouro de São Pedro de Alcântara. The rooms are small but adequately furnished; some have en-suite, others shared facilities. Breakfast included. 40 rooms.

Pensão Residencial Ninho das Aguias € *Costa do Castelo 74, tel: 218 854 070.* The 'eagle's nest' next to the castle is the most delightfully eccentric *pensão* in town. Not for the faint-hearted – you need to negotiate not just Alfama's cobbled streets but the building's rickety stairs, too. The rewards are wonderful: romantic terraces with great views. 17 rooms. Cash only.

Residencia Astória € *Rua Braancamp 10, tel: 213 861 317, fax: 213 860 491, <www.evidenciahoteis.com>.* The handsome exterior may outclass the rooms, but this mid-size, 1920s-style hotel in an elite part of town, just off Praça Marquês de Pombal, ranks as a bargain. Popular with both backpackers and older travellers looking for a deal. Rooms are plain but comfortable. 30 rooms.

Ritz Four Seasons Hotel Lisboa €€€€€ *Rua Rodrigo da Fonseca 88, tel: 213 814 400, fax: 213 831 783, <www.fourseasons.com>.* One of Lisbon's oldest luxury hotels certainly has pedigree in its names. Its ugly Soviet-style exterior could not be a greater contrast to its swanky interior, which was recently remodelled and is the height of indulgence. Rooms with balconies with good views over Parque Eduardo VII and busy Pombal square. Excellent restaurant, Veranda. Wheelchair access. 284 rooms.

Solar dos Mouros €€€–€€€€ *Rua Milagre de Santo António 6, tel: 218 854 940, fax: 218 854 945, <www.solardosmouros.com>*. A stylish boutique hotel up near the castle, occupying a tangerine-coloured renovated town house and enjoying panoramic views over the Tagus and city. The starkly modern rooms are individually designed with African art and genuine works by contemporary artists; they also feature marble bathrooms and hardwood floors. 12 rooms.

VIP Executive Suites Éden €€ *Praça dos Restauradores 24, tel: 213 216 600, fax: 213 216 666, <www.viphotels.com>*. In a famous Art Deco building right on Praça dos Restauradores, this cool, modern apartment-hotel is a great deal, especially for families. There are kitchen-equipped studios and full apartments, with daily or weekly maid service. Panoramic pool and breakfast service. Wheelchair access. 134 rooms.

York House €€€€ *Rua das Janelas Verdes 32, tel: 213 962 435, fax: 213 972 793, <www.yorkhouselisboa.com>*. Located near the Museu de Arte Antiga in Lapa, several blocks west of the centre, this converted 17th-century convent overlooks the River Tagus. It retains the feel of a serene retreat from the outside world, and rooms are elegant but not stuffy. Outdoor dining in the garden courtyard during the summer and a recommended on-premises restaurant. Wheelchair access. 34 rooms.

ESTORIL COAST

Hotel Albatroz €€€€ *Rua Frederico Arouca 100, Cascais, tel: 214 847 380, fax: 214 844 827, <www.albatrozhotels.com>*. This mansion perched above the Praia da Rainha beach is Cascais's most elegant hotel. Public rooms and accommodation swim in luxury. The Albatroz recently expanded into another beautiful palace across the street. Outdoor pool and good restaurant with superb views. 46 rooms.

Hotel Fortaleza do Guincho €€€€–€€€€€ *Estrada do Guincho, Cascais, tel: 214 870 491, fax: 214 870 431, <www.guinchotel.pt>.* Just outside of Cascais, in a former 16th-century fortress perched on a rocky ledge overlooking Guincho beach and the sea, this enchanting hotel is a remarkable getaway. Marvellous antique touches throughout, including tile floors and period silver and crystal. Most rooms have fireplaces, and many have balconies with views of the sea – including Cabo da Roca, Europe's westernmost point. 36 rooms.

Hotel Palácio do Estoril €€€ *Rua do Parque, Estoril, tel: 214 680 400, fax: 214 684 867, <www.palacioestorilhotel.com>.* This luxury hotel, established in 1930, looks like a cruise ship and is as palatial as its name suggests. Has undergone a major renovation. Heated outdoor pool, tennis courts and gardens. Special rates for guests at its golf course. Top-notch restaurant, Four Seasons. Wheelchair access. 162 rooms.

QUELUZ AND SINTRA

Pousada de D. Maria I €€–€€€ *Largo do Palácio, Edifício da Torre, Queluz, tel: 214 356 158, fax: 214 356 189, <www.pousadas.pt>.* Occupying the part of the royal summer palace that was the domain of the Royal Guard of the Court, this pink *pousada* is ideal if you want to explore Lisbon and its surroundings but aren't really keen on staying in the city. The rooms are attractive and well sized, and Cozinha Velha, the restaurant that's part of the palace across the road and is now associated with the government-owned *pousada*, is one of the area's best. 26 rooms.

Quinta da Capela €€€ *Estrada Velha de Colares, Sintra, tel: 219 290 170, fax: 219 293 425, <www.quintadacapela.com>.* A beautiful, rambling 16th-century house on an old country estate, 3km (2 miles) outside Sintra. Seven handsome, understated rooms in the main house, and three private cottages with self-catering. The gorgeous grounds, home to swans and peacocks, are ideal for a relaxed retreat. The chapel is still used for mass on Sunday. No restaurant. Closed November–March (cottages open year-round). 11 rooms.

Tivoli Palácio de Seteais €€€€–€€€€€ *Rua Barbosa do Bocage 10, Sintra, tel: 219 233 200, fax: 219 234 277, <www.tivoli hotels.com>.* A luxury hotel in a beautiful, 18th-century palace with antique furniture, manicured gardens and superb views. Some visitors find it a little dainty compared to more relaxed *quintas* nearby. Lord Byron wrote in the gardens here. Sports facilities include tennis courts and an outdoor pool. Horse riding. 30 rooms.

SOUTH OF LISBON

Pousada de Palmela €€€ *Castelo de Palmela, Palmela, tel: 212 351 226, fax: 212 330 440, <www.pousadas.pt>.* A luxury *pousada* carved out of a 12th-century hilltop castle, later a headquarters of the Order of Santiago, with a quiet cloister. Fabulous views towards Setúbal and the sea. Notable restaurant in the former refectory serving local dishes, especially seafood. 28 rooms.

Pousada de São Filipe €€€ *Forte de São Filipe, Setúbal, tel: 265 550 070, fax: 265 539 240, <www.pousadas.pt>.* A *pousada* inside the walls of a fortress built in 1590, overlooking the port of Setúbul. Great views of the Sado estuary and Tróia peninsula. Some rooms in the former castle's dungeons. Close to the Serra de Arrábida National Park. 14 rooms.

Quinta das Torres €€€ *Estrada Nacional 10, Vila Nogueira de Azeitão, tel: 212 180 001, fax: 212 190 607.* A 16th-century mansion with lived-in charm, 15km (9 miles) outside of Setúbal amid peaceful, relaxing grounds. The delightful rooms have ceramic tiles, religious art and antiques. Two suites have private terraces and fireplaces, and there are two private bungalows, with kitchens, that sleep four. 12 rooms.

Sana Sesimbra Hotel €€€ *Avenida 25 de Abril, Sesimbra, tel: 212 289 000, fax: 212 289 001, <www.sanahotels.com>.* Modern, stylish hotel just across the road from the main beach. Facilities include a restaurant and bar, as well as a rooftop pool with panoramic views of the bay. 100 rooms.

Recommended Restaurants

The Lisbon dining scene has become much more diverse in recent years. The Bairro Alto is still one of the best areas for eating out, since it's densest with restaurants of all kinds, especially small traditional dives. But as Lisbon moves to embrace the river again, restaurants have been popping up along the old dock areas – Doca de Alcântara, Doca do Poço do Bispo and Doca Jardim do Tabaco – and along the riverfront near the Parque das Nações, where Expo 98 was held.

Even the top restaurants in Lisbon are fairly affordable by the standards of European capitals. The 'tourist menu' (*ementa turística*) in many restaurants, especially at lunchtime, can be an excellent value at 10–15 euros with either wine, beer, mineral water or a soft drink included.

The prices indicated are for starter, main course and dessert, with wine, per person. (Note that some fish or shellfish dishes will be more expensive.) Tax (IVA) is included. All restaurants listed here accept major credit cards. Note that many Lisbon restaurants close for the entire month of August.

€€€€	over 40 euros
€€€	25–40 euros
€€	15–25 euros
€	below 15 euros

LISBON

BAIRRO ALTO

Cervejeria da Trindade €–€€ *Rua Nova da Trindade 20, tel: 213 423 506.* Open daily for lunch and dinner (until late). A famous old beer hall and restaurant, in a former monastery decorated with *azulejo*-covered walls. Extremely popular Portuguese cooking and seafood specialities at good prices; light bar snacks also available.

Pap 'Açorda €€–€€€ *Rua da Atalaia 57–9, tel: 213 464 811.* Open Tuesday–Saturday for lunch and dinner; Monday, dinner only. One of Lisbon's hippest spots, cool but disarmingly informal and popular with a wide-ranging clientele. Traditional and creative Portuguese dishes with fabulous and filling *açorda real* (a thick shellfish stew with lobster and shrimp) as the main speciality. Attentive service.

Principe do Calhariz €–€€ *Calçada do Combro 28–30, tel: 213 420 971.* Open Sunday–Friday for lunch and dinner. Lively restaurant just beyond the Bica funicular, this is a good place to discover local dishes, particularly from northern Portugal where the owners come from. Try *coelho à caçador* (rabbit, hunter's style).

Tavares Rico €€€–€€€€ *Rua da Misericórdia 37, tel: 213 421 112.* Open Monday–Friday for lunch and dinner; Saturday, dinner only. A stylish and immensely popular restaurant-café with ornate ceilings, mirrors and chandeliers. Classic French cuisine has been served here for more than a century.

CENTRAL LISBON

Alcântara Café €€€€ *Rua Maria Luísa Holstein 15, tel: 213 637 176.* Open daily for dinner. One of the restaurants of the moment, this handsome place, equal parts industrial and post-modern, is the goal of many of Lisbon's socialites. The menu is unique, but receives some mixed reports. Still, customers get what they come for – buzz.

Bica do Sapato €€€ *Avenida Infante D. Henrique (Cais da Pedra), tel: 218 810 320.* Open daily for lunch and dinner. Trendy restaurant in an old warehouse on the waterfront across from Santa Apolónia station. The funky decor is cool but not overdone. Excellent and fairly priced creative Portuguese menu and a good list of local wines.

Bonjardim € *Travessa de Santo Antão 10, tel: 213 427 424.* Open daily for lunch and dinner. In a street full of restaurants near Rossio, this large and lively place is terrific for low-key, filling and dirt-cheap Portuguese cooking. The roasted chicken with crisp fries seems to be the signature dish. Annex across the street.

Café-Café €€€ *Rua de Cascais 31, tel: 213 610 310.* Open Monday–Saturday for dinner. Giving Alcântara Café a run for its money as a beacon for beautiful people, Café-Café draws crowds with its sleek modernist design and Portuguese nouvelle cuisine. The bar is on the first floor, the restaurant on the second, where tables surround a grand piano. Major credit cards.

Casa da Comida €€€€ *Travessa das Amoreiras 1, tel: 213 885 376.* Open Monday–Friday for lunch and dinner, Saturday dinner only. An elegant but not stuffy, handsomely decorated restaurant in northwest Lisbon near the aqueduct. Fine Portuguese and French cuisine served outdoors in a patio setting in an old mansion. A good place to blow the bank.

A Confraria €€€ *Rua das Janelas Verdes 32 (in York House hotel), tel: 213 962 435.* Open daily for lunch and dinner. Inhabiting the former 17th-century convent of the refined and retreat-like York House, this is a cut above a typical hotel restaurant. Eugénia Cerqueira creates a daily menu with imaginative interpretations of Portuguese cuisine. The classic-looking restaurant spills out onto a beautiful, quiet courtyard. Excellent desserts.

Gambrinus €€€€ *Rua das Portas de Santo Antão 25, tel: 213 421 466.* Open daily for lunch and dinner (until late). A sophisticated and elegant restaurant, one of the city's finest and most famous, in this street of restaurants. Specialises in traditional Portuguese and Galician dishes, which means fresh seafood.

Leão d'Ouro €€€ *Rua de Dezembro 105, tel: 213 426 195.* Open daily for lunch and dinner. Big, bright, centrally situated, *azulejo*-lined restaurant, dating from 1640, just off the Rossio. Seafood is the speciality. Try the *cataplana* fish stew or the seafood rice with shrimp, lobster, mussels and prawns.

Martinho da Arcada €€€ *Arcadas do Terreiro do Paço/Praça do Comércio 3, tel: 218 879 259.* Open Monday–Saturday for lunch and dinner. Lisbon's oldest café, under the arcades at Praça do Comércio, dates back to 1778 and has a colourful history littered with political and literary figures – try the Menu Fernando Pessoa. Today, it is a national monument and still a great, atmospheric place for a bite to eat.

Tágide €€€€ *Largo da Academia Nacional de Belas Artes 18, tel: 213 404 010.* Open Sunday–Friday for lunch and dinner. Classic Portuguese and French restaurant west of the Praça do Comércio in an elegant, old house offering magnificent views of the waterfront, cathedral and square. Popular with the expense-account crowd.

A Travessa €€€ *Travessa Convento Bernardas 12, tel: 213 902 034.* Open Monday–Saturday for lunch and dinner. A Belgian- and French-influenced menu with dishes such as mussels, stuffed aubergine and bacon-wrapped dates enlivens this good-looking place near Parliament. Mussel feasts on Saturday nights.

ALFAMA

Casa do Leão €€ *Castelo de São Jorge, tel: 218 875 962.* Open daily for lunch and dinner. The only restaurant located just inside the castle ramparts and serving a wide range of traditional international and Portuguese dishes. Excellent views.

Flor dos Arcos € *Largo do Chafariz de Dentro 11, tel: 218 872 035.* Open daily for lunch and dinner. This tourist-friendly budget restaurant on the corner of Chafariz de Dentro will give you a good introduction to the Alfama: bars and *fado* houses lead on from here.

BÉLEM

O Caseiro € *Rua de Belém 35, tel: 213 638 803.* Open Monday–Saturday for lunch and dinner. Closed August. In a convenient location between the Coach Museum and the monastery, this is an informal but intimate restaurant serving simple but tasty local dishes. Specialities include *porco á alentejana* (pork, Alentejo style).

A Commenda €€€ *Praça do Império, Belém (inside the Belém Cultural Centre), tel: 213 627 327, 213 612 400.* Closed Sunday dinner. Fine river views top the sophisticated atmosphere of this excellent restaurant. Good traditional Portuguese food. The Sunday 'brunch' is famous and includes fruit juices, bacon and eggs and a glass of champagne.

São Jerónimo €€ *Rua dos Jerónimos 12, tel: 213 648 796.* Open Monday–Friday for lunch and dinner, Saturday for dinner only. A sleek, beautifully designed restaurant with warm woods, attractive dimmed lighting and leather chairs, just around the corner from the Jerónimos Monastery. The menu is creative Portuguese.

PARQUE DAS NAÇÕES

O Nobre €€€€ *Edificio Nau, Marina Expo 98, tel: 218 931 600.* Open Monday–Saturday for lunch and dinner. Long one of Lisbon's top restaurants, O Nobre opened in the Marina of the Parque das Nações without losing a step, continuing a tradition of exquisite, classic Portuguese cooking with professional and attentive. O Nobre Buffet is less formal. Its sister restaurant of the same name is in Rua das Mercês 71, in Ajuda.

Restaurante Panorâmico Torre Vasco da Gama €€€€ *Parque das Nações, tel: 218 939 550.* Closed Monday. Reservations essential. Luxury restaurant serving Portuguese and international cuisine, near the top of Lisbon's tallest building. Spectacular views over the river and the Vasco da Gama bridge.

THE DOCKS

Price ranges are the average for restaurants in the Docks.

Doca do Alcântara €€–€€€ *By Alcântara train station.* Next door to the Doco Santo Amaro, the main passenger dock's nightlife includes Dock's Club and Blues Cafe. Floating restaurants, such as A Fragate Batelhão Afonso d'Alburqueque and O Barqueria are popular for business lunches and evening pleasure-seakers.

Doca do Bom Sucesso €€€–€€€€ *Belém.* This small marina in Belém has become a popular nightlife spot for business people and politicos. Restaurants are predictably upmarket and fashionable, including Vela Latina and Spazio Evasione.

Doca Jardim do Tabaco €€–€€€ *Avenida Infante D. Henrique, Pavilhão A–B, tel: 218-824 280.* Between Casa dos Bicos and Santa Apolónia railway station is a series of popular docks converted into restaurants. They look out over the Tagus as well as the Alfama district. Restaurants include Jardim do Marisco and Rodizio.

Doca de Santo Amaro €€€–€€€€ *Alcântara Mar.* On the Rio Tejo near the 25 de Abril bridge, Doca de Santo Amaro is the best-known dock and has a lively bar-and-restaurant scene. Most places open daily for lunch and dinner. The best idea is to stroll along the dock and choose a restaurant that looks appealing. Some to keep an eye out for include: Café In (Avenida de Brasilia 311); Doca 6 (Armazém 6); Doca Peixe (Armazém 14) and Doca de Santo (Armazém CP).

OUTSIDE LISBON

Colares Velho €€–€€€ *Largo Dr Carlos França 1–4, Colares (Sintra), tel: 219 292 406.* Open daily for lunch and dinner. Closed Monday. A lovely, small restaurant in the village of Colares, several kilometres down the mountain road from Sintra. The dining room is like the library of a country estate. Dishes are imaginative and professionally done. Homemade desserts and good daily specials.

Cozinha Velha €€€ *Palácio Nacional de Queluz, Largo do Palácio, Queluz, tel: 214 350 232.* Open daily for lunch and dinner. One of the most atmospheric restaurants in Portugal, this was once the old kitchen of the royal palace. It has a garden patio and a decor that will transport you to the 17th century. The regional cooking is excellent.

Lawrence Hotel €€€€ *Rua Consigliéri Pedrosa 38–40, Sintra; tel 219 230 963.* Open daily for lunch and dinner. The Dutch owners call this 'a restaurant with rooms' rather than a hotel, and Portugal's prime minister is among many who declare it their favourite place to eat. Opened in 1764, it's the oldest hotel in Portugal (Byron stayed here in 1809), and its restaurant is renowned.

INDEX

Alfama 26–33
Antigua Casa de Pastéis
    de Belém 46
Aqueduto das Águas
    Livres 56–7
Atlântico Hall 60
Avenida da Liberdade 39
Azurra Palace 27

Bairro Alto 40–4
Baixa 35–9
Beco da Cardosa 29
Beco do Carneiro 29
Belém 46–52
Boca do Inferno 74

Cabo Espichel 77
Cabo da Roca 75
Café A Brasileira 43
Casa do Alentejo 38–9
Casa dos Bicos 33
Casa do Fado e
    da Guitarra
    Portuguesa 26
Cascais 73–4
Castelo dos Mouros 67
Castelo de São Jorge 31–2
Cathedral
    see Sé Patriarcal
Cemitério dos Ingleses 44
Centro de Arte Moderna
    56
Centro Cultural de
    Belém 50
Cervejeria da Trindade
    42
Chiado 43–4
Cristo Rei, statue of 61

Doca do Alcântara 46
Doca de Santo Amaro 46

Elevador de Glória 40
Elevador de Santa Justa
    36–7
Ericeira 70–1
Estação do Oriente 58
Estação do Rossio 39
Estoril 71–2
Estufa Fria 53
Estufa Quente 53

Fragata D. Fernando II
    e Glória 46

Guincho 75

Igreja do Carmo 42–3
Igreja de Jesus 78
Ireja de Santo António
    da Sé 33
Igreja de Santo Estêvão
    28–9
Ireja de São Miguel 28
Igrcja de São Roque 41
Igreja e Mosteiro de São
    Vicente de Fora 29

Jardim Botânico 41
Jardim da Estrela 44

Lapa 44–6
Largo Barão Quintela 43
Largo das Portas do Sol
    27
Largo de São Rafael 28
Lisboa Welcome Centre
    36

Miradouro de Santa
    Luzia 26–7
Miradouro de São Pedro
    de Alcântara 40

Mosteiro dos Jerónimos
    47–50
Museu de Água 56
Museu de Arte
    Sacra 42
Museu de Artes
    Decorativas 27–8
Museu do Chiado 43
Museu de Cidade
    (Setúbal) 78
Museu dos Condes de
    Castro Guimarães
    (Cascais) 74
Museu Gulbenkian 53–5
Museu do Mar –
    Rei Dom Carlos
    (Cascais) 78
Museu da Marinha 50
Museu Militar 33–4
Museu Nacional de
    Arqueologia 49–50
Museu Nacional de
    Arte Antiga 44–6
Museu Nacional
    del Azulejo 34
Museu Nacional dos
    Coches 47

Oceanário de Lisboa 59

Paços do Concelho
    (Cascais) 73
Padrão dos
    Descobrimentos 50–1
Palácio da Ajuda 52
Palácio Foz 39
Palácio da Pena 67–8
Palácio Nacional de
    Mafra 69–70
Palácio Nacional
    de Queluz 62–4

Palácio Nacional de
    Sintra 65–6
Palácio São Bento 44
Panteão Nacional 30
Parque Eduardo VII 52–3
Parque das Nações
    58–61
Parque Natural da
    Arrábida 77
Pavilhão do
    Conhecimento 60
Planetário 50
Ponte 25 de Abril 61
Portinho da Arrábida 77
Portugal Pavilion 61
Praça do Comércio 35–6
Praça da Figueira 39

Praça Marquês de
    Pombal 39
Praça Martim Moniz 39
Praça dos Restauradores
    39

Quinta da Regaleira 68

Rossio 37–8
Rua Augusta 36
Rua dos Bacalhoeiros 33
Rua do Carmo 37
Rua Garrett 43
Rua das Portas
    de Santo Antão 38
Rua de São João da
    Praça 28

Rua de São Pedro 28

Sé Patriarcal 32
Serra da Arrábida 76–7
Serra de Sintra 75
Sesimbra 75–6
Setúbal 78
Sintra 64–9
Solar do Vinho do Porto
    40–1

Teatro Camões 60
Teatro Nacional
    Dona Maria II 38
Torre de Belém 51–2
Torre Vasco da Gama
    58, 60

Berlitz pocket guide

Lisbon

Fourth Edition 2008
Reprinted 2008

Written by Neil Schlecht
Revised by Roger Williams
Updated by Marion Kaplan
Series Editor: Tony Halliday

All Rights Reserved
© 2008 Berlitz Publishing/Apa
Publications GmbH & Co. Verlag KG,
Singapore Branch, Singapore

Printed in Singapore by Insight Print
Services (Pte) Ltd, 38 Joo Koon Road,
Singapore 628990. Tel: (65) 6865-1600.
Fax: (65) 6861-6438

Berlitz Trademark Reg. U.S. Patent Office
and other countries. Marca Registrada

Photography credits
akg-images London 55; Bridgeman Art Library
45; Chris Coe 16, 94; Tony Halliday 1, 6, 8, 10,
11, 12, 19, 20, 24, 27, 28, 31, 32, 33, 34–5, 37,
38, 41, 42, 51, 52, 53, 56–7, 58, 60, 65, 66, 68,
69, 70, 71, 72, 73, 74, 75, 76, 77, 79, 82, 84, 89,
92; Claude Huber 91; Lisbon Tourist Board 22,
47, 48, 80, 83, 87, 96, 99; Museu Nacional de
Arte Antiga, Lisbon 15; Ingolf Pompe/Impact
40; Neil Schlecht 43, 63; Phil Wood 101; Ernst
Wrba/Alamy Images 59

Cover picture: Grant Faint/Getty Images

Contact us

At Berlitz we strive to keep our guides as
accurate and up to date as possible, but if you
find anything that has changed, or if you have
any suggestions on ways to improve this guide,
then we would be delighted to hear from you.

Berlitz Publishing, PO Box 7910,
London SE1 1WE, England
fax: (44) 20 7403 0290
email: berlitz@apaguide.co.uk
www.berlitzpublishing.com